Diego Armando
Maradona

1960-2020

By Harry Harris

Foreword by Ossie Ardiles

"He leaves us but does not leave, because Diego is eternal."
LIONEL MESSI

"One day we'll kick a ball together in the sky above."

PELE

Published 2021
© G2 Entertainment 2021
www.g2books.co.uk

ISBN 978-1-782811-62-6

CONTENTS

ABOUT THE AUTHOR

Few journalists have ever enjoyed such a remarkable one-to-one interview with Diego Maradona in his life time. Harry Harris was there.

He was there in the Azteca Stadium to watch Diego Maradona score his wonder goal four minutes after the infamous Hand of God goal. He interviewed the late Bobby Robson minutes after the final whistle. He can also count Ossie Ardiles among his closest confidantes in football, and has interviewed the man who knows Diego best since the premature and tragic death at the age of 60. Most remarkably, he shared a car ride to the Lane with Ossie and Diego in one of the most unusual personal interviews Maradona has ever given any journalist, especially one from England.

Harry was also there for the World Cup in the United States in 1994 and raced across the country to be at the Dallas press conference when he witnessed more global media than he had ever seen in his 40-year career as one of the UK's most prominent journalists, after Maradona's positive drug test, when he was kicked out of the tournament.

Harry has written as astonishing 80 books, including biographies of superstars such as Pele, Ruud Gullit, George Best, Jurgen Klinsmann, Glenn Hoddle, Franco Zola and Wayne Rooney. Now he has focused on the remarkable life and times of Diego Maradona.

Harry Harris (left), with Diego Maradona and his first wife Claudia Villafane, and Ossie Ardiles - 1986

A TRIBUTE BY OSSIE ARDILES

All our conversations would finish in the same way… He would say it is very beautiful to be Maradona, but it is not easy to be Maradona.

First of all, it was a big, big shock when I heard the news of his passing. In many ways, it was news I had been expecting at some point but when it happened it was an incredible shock, whether I was prepared for it or not. A week earlier Ray Clemence passed away, and then Diego. It was a very sad time.

For me, Diego was one of the three I would always pick out as the very best in the history of the game. There are, of course, more players I could mention, but there are three when I ever mention the all-time greats — Pele, Maradona, and Messi. Of those three, Diego is the best.

Like Pelé, Diego played at a time when it was much more difficult to play than now. Now nobody is allowed to touch you, but when Diego played there was always the chance of being injured, and it was always a question of when you would be hurt — and hurt by what I would call 'the bad boys', who were out to catch him.

It might have been incredibly difficult at the time he played, but he was extraordinarily skilful, tremendously gifted, an unbelievable talent. What would he be worth now? Even at that time he was the most expensive transfer of all time, and he would be the most expensive transfer now.

He will be remembered as a genius in football. You can see the extraordinary amount of interest that he generates. People like Ronaldo, or people like Messi, they couldn't even dream of having this kind of admiration. That was the Maradona phenomenon - all the time.

Diego came from Villa Fiorito on the outskirts of Buenos Aires. It's not quite a shanty town but it's very close to that. It was a poor background. In Argentinian football we have this myth about 'El Pibe' or the boy. It is the little, skilful boy footballer who succeeds against all the odds and makes it big, that is the legend behind 'El Pibe'. It's part of our culture. And Diego fulfilled that role absolutely. From where he was born, there was a sense of being against the law. It was a world where the police were the bad guys and the criminals were heroes, because you had to survive however you could. This is what Diego was. He had to survive and he would be prepared to do anything to do that. And survival for him was to win the game. And he would do anything to do it. Despite his background, money didn't really interest him. To be honest, he didn't need it. Wherever he went, everything was paid for him. Wherever he went they gave him a car or a watch... he would have one hundred watches at home, all better than the other. He never needed anything. He didn't carry cash. What for? But there were many people in his life who exploited that and cheated him but he never forgot his background and he felt at peace with the fans and poor people. He was a hero for them and they identified with them. Presidents and kings would invite him and he would refuse. Or he would go and keep them waiting, arriving one hour late. He was always fighting with powers that be, presidents of Argentina, the Pope, presidents of the USA, the FIFA president and people identified with him. I've seen this in India, in Jordan, in Japan. And in Latin America he was hugely popular because of what he represented. Only our former president, Juan Peron and his wife Eva Peron — Evita — have come close to his popularity with the poor. People wouldn't really appreciate the intelligence of Diego unless you shared a dressing room with him. He was incredibly sharp with the banter. There was no point getting into a verbal contest with him. You couldn't get the last word, he would always answer you back in a way that meant he won the argument. He was a graduate of the university of the street.

He always wanted to know things, especially about Europe. In Argentina at the time, they looked down on European football. The general feeling was 'they're strong, they run like mad but they can't play' but he wanted to know about Europe and at this time he was about to move to Barcelona, so he would ask me. He was humble despite being Diego. When we watched football on the TV in camp and someone made a mistake, he never joined in the laughter or mockery and he had an extraordinary respect for the guys of the 1978 team. He once picked his all-time Argentinian XI and six were from the 1978 team [Ardiles was one of them].

My first memory of him was some time before this. Back in 1975, when we were playing with the national side at Boca Juniors stadium, La Bombonera, they would get a child to entertain the crowd before the game. This kid was at Argentinos Juniors, but he hadn't made his debut. He was 14 or 15 years old but he was already a minor celebrity, juggling the ball before the games. And, to be honest, he was fantastic. We were national team players but we would go out to see him perform. He would be walking around the stadium with the ball, doing these extraordinary tricks as he talked to people and waved to the crowd. We were saying to each other: 'How can he even do this?' That was how I met my lifelong friend, Diego Maradona. For the last few days I have been thinking about all the memories I have of him and thinking back to that time when he was a child. Within a year, we would meet him again at training for the national team. He was 15 or 16 by then. Cesar Menotti, our manager, would always bring a couple of young players into the sessions to make up the numbers, so that we could play 11 a side. The day came when Diego showed up, very humble, a bit nervous. To be honest, he was in awe of us. He was still a child, already a little bit stocky. You can imagine how sceptical we were. Of course, as soon as he played, we could see how good he was. He was a sensation. But you know footballers. They can be very cynical. We had seen so many young players who were extremely skilful but never made it. He was more skilful than any other but there was still this doubt. And we were saying: "Well, of course, he's very good. But look at him! He's too small! He will never make it. We're talking about playing in the Argentinian first team." This wasn't football for creative players. It was football for the baddies. Within a year, he had made his debut for the national team at the age of 16, when he came on for Leopoldo Luque against Hungary in 1977. And after that he was one of us.

The 1978 World Cup was approaching and it would be hosted in Argentina. Because of that, 25 players were taken out of club football and went to a training camp to work together for six months from January 1978. It was obvious he was brilliant. But I think it created a problem for Menotti. During difficult times in 1976-77, he had promised the squad of 22 that he would stick by us for the World Cup because we had stuck by him. And I don't think he felt he could break that promise. And that is why, at the end of April 1978, Diego was one of the players left out. This has been on my mind ever since the news of his death came through. That day Diego was crying as he left the hotel. We couldn't comfort him. We were saying: 'Diego you're young. You'll have other chances.' But he carried on crying and crying. By the end, all of us were crying. For Diego, it was the biggest setback he suffered as a footballer. He had some wonderful moments and some bad moments in his career but that was the biggest shock of his footballing life.

When we played in the 1978 World Cup, the team that started the tournament was pretty much the team that played and won in the final apart from one position, where we struggled to find a solution: the No 10. We started with Jose Daniel Valencia, we had Norberto Alonso, we had Ricky Villa and we finished with Mario Kempes, a centre forward, playing there. What might we have been like with Diego? Soon after 1978 he was recognised as the best player in the world and when he was with the national team he would almost do the same as he had done as a 14-year-old boy before the matches. Only this time he was a player and it was part of his warm-up. He would stand in the middle of the pitch and start juggling the ball. Then he would kick the ball up in the air and begin chatting to you as though he had forgotten it. 'Ossie, how are you today?' And then 'Boom!'. The ball would fall on to his foot again as though he knew exactly where it was all the time. It is impossible to do that! I haven't seen anyone do anything close to that! He would do that knowing that the other team was there. Most of the time, the opponents stopped their warm-up to watch, knowing that ten minutes later they would be playing this monster. He knew that and did it to give us the advantage. For the other team it was: 'Blimey!' And for us playing with him, it was: 'Hello! He's playing for us! No problems.'

Diego was unique, that is the word. He was extraordinary, out of this world. He had feet like hands. I was blessed to play with the world's best players, but he was the greatest. What made him so special was his courage. It was always hostile for him, he was always a marked man but he always wanted the ball. They kicked him - he wanted the ball even more. He was a winner. He just could not lose. And I should know, I played him at tennis!

There is one story I have never told about Diego. It happened in the 1982 World Cup in Spain and we travelled to a small town in Spain about 10 days before the tournament. I was sitting next to Diego at dinner, when he asked me what I was doing the next day. It was an unusual situation as we also had our wives, and in Diego's case, his girlfriend, staying in the next hotel. That never used to happen as we were happy just to concentrate on the tournament. It was a Saturday evening when he asked me about my plans for the next day. "Cordobes, what are you doing tomorrow?" he said. He called me that because I was from the town of Cordoba in Argentina. We woke the next morning and, after a quick breakfast, we slipped past all the security that was around us due to the war with England over the Falklands, pinched a car outside of the hotel, as there were so many there, and headed into town — about a 15-minute drive away to go to mass and have some lunch afterwards.

We went to this small cathedral and when we opened the door everybody looked at us, the priest had to stop the mass, as everybody wanted to touch Diego, or have a picture with him, as even then, he was so well known. The priest took us into a corner but Diego said it was no problem if anyone wanted a picture.

During the mass, you would turn to the person next to you and say "Peace is with you", and put your hand in their hand — and sitting next to us was someone from England! Incredible. Back at the hotel, we heard later, there was panic. "Where are Diego and Ossie?" Back at the cathedral, before mass had finished, at the door were some big guards in sunglasses, "Oh, there they are!" We took our car back to the hotel accompanied by security.

For the 1982 World Cup, we were favourites and were confident. Basically we had the core of the '78 team which were world champions, with Jorge Valdano, Ramon Diaz and Diego. We fancied ourselves very strongly but immediately things started to go wrong. And the main thing was the war with England over Las Malvinas/The Falkland Islands. Because of the way the news was reported in Argentina under the dictatorship, when we left Argentina everyone had the impression that we were winning the war. When we arrived in Spain, we had surrendered. That was an incredible shock. Some of us had family and friends in the war and I had a cousin who had died there. We had a team meeting and said: 'Boys, the best way to help the country is to win the World Cup.' All the time, it was at the back of our minds. We lost against Belgium in the first game and we ended up in the Group of Death with eventual champions Italy and the Brazil team, which is the greatest Brazilian team not to win the World Cup.

Against Italy, they just lined up to kick Diego and we lost 2-1. Against Brazil he was also marked in a very physical way and, when he reacted, he was sent off - we lost that one 3-1. We had taken on all the pressure and responsibility for the nation from the war, Diego more than most, and it proved too much. Daniel Passarella may have been our captain but Diego was the leader. There was too much on his shoulders. But throughout his life, there was always too much on his shoulders. On the plane home, I told him, "Diego, they will destroy us. The criticism will be so big. And you will be the one who will be criticised more than anyone. Because you are the best player in the world and you didn't perform. And you were sent off." He knew that. And it was exactly as we said. It was very difficult to take.

After the World Cup he left Argentina for Barcelona and there he received similar treatment, with that infamous tackle from Andoni Goikoetxea. If he had done that on the street it would have been a crime, but in the context of football at the time, it was OK. This was a career-threatening injury and Diego was out for half a season and at the end of that season he would move to Napoli a year before the 1986 World Cup finals. Can you believe that Naples would win Serie A? People laughed. Football was dominated by the north, by Juventus, AC Milan, Inter, Roma. It had never happened that Napoli could win the title.

It was during his time at Napoli, at the 1986 World Cup, that he cemented his legend. It's the tournament for which we will always remember him. I was injured and for that England game, I was an analyst for ITV. I saw the first goal and immediately I saw Glenn Hoddle, my team-mate at Spurs, and Steve Hodge protesting. I sensed something was wrong. It wasn't offside. I was puzzled. What could it be? I could see when Diego was celebrating, there was a quick look back in his eyes. And I thought: 'Uh, oh!' Only when we got a different angle could you see the hand. I know people will say: 'How could he do such a thing?' But these things happen in football all the time. As for the second goal, Diego has scored better goals than this but it is the occasion that makes that particular goal special. This was one of the most famous games in the history of the World Cup and that's why it is the goal of the century. And because of the burden he carried for Argentina for the defeat in the war. That's why he would never apologise for the handball. If it had been another opponent, maybe he would say sorry. But for him, it was personal.

In the lead up to that World Cup Diego was Argentina's big hope, but there were two very important warm-up games in Denmark and then Israel but after the Denmark game, Diego announced that he was off to London to play a game for Tottenham. Diego said to Carlos Bilardo, the manager, "By the way, I'm going to London for Ossie". Bilardo said, "What? You are joking, you're not going!". "No, I'm Diego Maradona, I'm going". They couldn't believe it, and told him, "No, you are not going." He told them: "I am going." They insisted he was not going. But he had told me he would play in my testimonial, so he left the World Cup camp and headed off to London even though he was not allowed to.

I picked him up at the airport and took him to a hotel in central London where he insisted he wanted a sleep before the game. I told him we must leave early as there would be a big crowd wanting to see him, and that it was always a lot of traffic. I waited for hours, and as he had his phone off the hook, could not get through to his room. He finally emerged with little to no time to get to the ground.

We inevitably got stuck in traffic and the kick off had to be put back, there was a full house.

I was panicking as I drove him along Seven Sisters Road which had come to a standstill, but we had a police escort for the final stages to get us to the stadium. He wanted to wear his famous No10, so Glenn gave him his No10 shirt. Diego had arrived without a thing, not even a bag, let alone any kit.

For him to come and wear a Spurs shirt and play that game for me, it was very special. He had a fantastic game, and after the game the team went to dinner with Diego, and then onto a private nightclub where I left him about three in the morning. He hardly had much sleep the night before travelling and not much sleep the next night but had to make it to the airport at 7am, and almost missed his flight to Israel, but I imagine he got some sleep on the flight.

I brought him to Wembley when Spurs played there and beat Liverpool 4-1 when Mauricio Pochettino was the manager, and all the players wanted to meet him. I introduced him to Harry Kane as he popped into the dressing room to say hello. He gave some advice to Harry Kane. I was translating, "Harry, when you shoot, look one way with your eyes, but shoot the other". But the way Diego talks, so passionate, so funny. Harry loved it.

Diego was a guest speaker at Oxford Union in 1995, when I was the interpreter. Here was Diego, on the same stage where Nelson Mandela and Ronald Reagan had stood. Suddenly, one guy shouts, "Can you do keepie-uppies with this?", and he throws a golf ball towards us. I'm thinking, "Oh no, he's wearing a suit and brand new shoes, this will be difficult". Diego pulls his trousers up and starts keeping the ball up. Boom, boom, boom. Easy. He then kicks it back to the guy with his heel. It was incredible. Only Diego.' The Union erupted with cheers.

Obviously everyone talks about the Hand of God goal, but he did what he had to do, and for me it is blown out of all proportion. Here we have a unique talent, who scored a wonder goal against England, but the Hand of God goal is the one they talk about. He wanted to win at all costs, do anything to win, he was a winner, but he wasn't the only forward who handled a goal, there are many other examples, from Thierry Henry to Joe Jordan, it happens all the time. I can't judge him on that. In the intervening years I have talked to Diego regularly, sometimes for five minutes, sometimes half an hour; we would talk about football, but we would talk about everything. I always tried to help him as much as I could.

At the 1990 World Cup finals, when Argentina lost in the final, Diego was in incredibly bad shape physically and to play every game he had cortisone injections. In 1994 it was the same. He was taking drugs to get him through games. So drugs were always there. There was no control in his life at that stage. And the only part of his life that was happy was on the pitch. It was sad to see him. He couldn't continue to live like that. He would always say: 'If I was a good boy and looked after myself, imagine the player I could be!' For him, a match was a show. At his best, he didn't need to warm up or concentrate. But before a game he would almost be in frenzy, using swear words to motivate himself and us. He would transmit just how much it meant to him. And the team would look at him and think: 'We have to play so well for him today.' He was our leader and that is how I will remember him.

All our conversations would finish in the same way... He would say "it is very beautiful to be Maradona, but it is not easy to be Maradona". I knew what he meant. He was loved wherever he went, no, more than loved, people absolutely loved him, wanted a part of him, a picture with him, just to touch him, and he was wonderful with the people. But he was mortal just like the rest of us, he never had a childhood because he was so famous so quickly. He came from a very poor background, but never forgot it, and the first thing he did when he could was to buy a house for his mother and father, and to make sure all his family were well looked after.

When you were with him, because he was such an icon, you were always surrounded by people. Things were always happened; exciting things. I loved him, absolutely loved him. He was incredibly sharp, very funny. He had an answer to whatever you said. But he had so many problems outside the pitch his entire life. Inside the pitch, he was the happiest person in the world.

Diego was an inspirational person. He had a magic around him, on the pitch and off it. Special, so special. I am blessed to have been his friend.

He didn't need to work, but the best thing for him was to be involved in football. When the pandemic happened, there has been no football in Argentina for six months. That did not help. He had been ill and he deteriorated badly. I am very sad, but now, he is in a place where he will find peace.

Osvaldo Ardiles

Ossie was one of the first to pay tribute to his ex-team-mate, tweeting: "Thank dear Dieguito for your friendship, for your football, sublime, without comparison. Simply the best football player in the history of football."

He tweeted posted a photo of himself and his two sons along with Maradona at White Hart Lane: "Diego with my two sons... still in shock. Very very sad but I'm sure Dieguito have peace now. Prayers and thoughts with his family and friends."

HERO OR VILLAIN?

This book sets out to trace Diego Maradona's exceptional life, both on and off the pitch, to decipher whether the genius on the pitch, but such a flawed character off the pitch, made him a hero or a villain.

I was there in the Azteca to witness the Hand of God goal, only a matter of weeks before having met him for the first time for an exclusive interview in the back of Ossie Ardiles' car as he drove us to White Hart Lane on the evening that Maradona donned Glenn Hoddle's no. 10 jersey and mesmerised the crowd.

The episode of how the three of us were stuck in traffic and Ossie feared they would never get there, which I expand upon in this book, is one of the personal recollections, and should be no surprise it is filled with drama and intrigue so fitting of Maradona's life story.

I was also there covering the World Cup in the USA when he failed a drugs test, and raced across several states to attend the media conference when FIFA announced his punishment – and experienced for the first time mass hysteria among the media attending – there was certainly no chance of any social distancing that day!

When Diego Maradona died aged 60, I was contacted by TalkSport, and a couple of newspapers, and wrote a first person article with Ossie for the *London Evening Standard*, and interviewed Peter Reid for the *Star on Sunday*. I had just completed a book with Peter and Steph Shilton was so fully aware of the feelings of England's record 125 cap goalkeeper who can neither forget or forgive the Hand of God goal.

Clearly, in his native Argentina, the people seemed willing to forgive all of Diego's flaws, of which, there were many. In England so many appreciated his extraordinary talents which put him on a different planet to other mere mortals, but equally the stigma of that Hand of God goal was never too far away form everyone's thoughts when he died at home a fortnight after leaving hospital following surgery for a blood clot in his brain.

Maradona underwent successful brain surgery, but was then undergoing treatment for alcohol dependency when nine ambulances were sent to his house in Buenos Aires.

One of the nurses caring for him raised the alarm after discovering Maradona had suffered a cardiac arrest at his home in Tigre. Local media said the preliminary results of an autopsy showed he had suffered "acute heart failure".

The last person to see Maradona alive was his nephew Johnny Esposito, according to statements gathered by officials. One of the greatest football players of all time endured a troubled personal life marked by obesity and cocaine and alcohol addiction. A spokesman told AFP news agency he would be laid to rest in a cemetery on the outskirts of Buenos Aires, where his parents were also buried.

As news of his death emerged stadiums across Argentina switched on their floodlights to honour his memory. Fans flocked to La Bombonera, Boca Juniors' stadium in Buenos Aires, where many were in tears. One fan of the star's former club had tears in his eyes as he explained how much Maradona meant to him. "Maradona for me is the greatest thing that happened to me in life. I love him as much as my father and it's like my old man died," Cristian Montelli, 22, told Reuters news agency. "If I die young, hopefully upstairs I can play ball and watch a Boca game with him."

Officials rushed to install cordons and other measures to try to limit the spread of coronavirus, as big crowds gathered on the Argentine capital's Plaza de Mayo after news of the death emerged. Late into the night, a sea of people in Argentina shirts thronged the streets across the country to mourn Maradona's death, and celebrate his life. Thousands of miles away in Italy, fans also gathered outside Napoli's San Paolo stadium, which was lit up in tribute to the man who scored 81 goals in 188 appearances for the club. Fireworks erupted in the sky as those below, clad in Maradona shirts and even Maradona face masks, chanted and wept. A minute's silence took place before Champions League matches and the same will happen before all other European fixtures this week.

For Argentinians, it was like the death of Princess Diana here in England, an outpouring of national grief right across the country, and in many ways there was a similarity in their vulnerability as well as their iconic status. Yet for every glorious trophy and on the field success, there was off the field torment and brush with the football authorities.

Maradona never had the best relationship, either, with the media. There's one instance of journalists getting a slap on the cheek for asking what he deemed a stupid question, and no doubt there were many more where the media chose to turn the other cheek!

But Maradona, being Maradona, took things to another level in February 1994 when he injured four reporters by shooting at them with an air rifle. In an incident of sheer madness, captured by television cameras for posterity, Maradona emerged from his country home near Buenos Aires to confront the press pack camped assembled outside. Crouching behind a Mercedes car with two other men, he started firing the gun at the crowd of reporters. Those injured sued Maradona but it took four years for the case to be heard with the player given a two-year suspended sentence. After 40 years in journalism, I can imagine quite a few who would like to take a pot shot at the media, but never to this extreme!

It happened when Maradona's life was in a downward spiral at the time and a few months later he would be sent home in disgrace from the 1994 World Cup after testing positive for a banned drug.

But that wasn't Maradona's last run-in with the press. On the day Maradona, as manager of Argentina, named his 23-man squad for the 2010 World Cup in South Africa, while driving in a Mini to the press conference to make the announcement he was mobbed and accidentally drove over a cameraman's foot amid the scrum. Of course, the accident wasn't his fault, as he made clear to the stricken man. 'What an a★★hole you are. How can you put your leg there when it can get run over, man?'

Maradona's career was almost over by the time of the failed drug test, and his early departure from the 1994 World Cup after testing positive for the banned stimulant Ephedrine but he wouldn't depart the international stage until having given the world one final reminder of his enduring sublime talents and world class skills. Maradona scored a stunning goal in Argentina's 4-0 win over Greece in their opening group match in Foxborough, in a World Cup tournament in which England didn't even qualify and poor old Graham Taylor paid the price with his job as England manager. What followed was one of the World Cup's most infamous celebrations as he ran towards a pitchside TV camera shouting at the top of his voice with his eyes bulging and face distorted, and it was pretty clear to the watching millions that they great player was also on something special to reach such highs. Little wonder he ended up on FIFA's hit list of 'random' drug tests after games.

Even though no longer prominently involved, Maradona's executive box antics became an entertaining sideshow to Argentina's matches at the 2018 World Cup in Russia with the TV cameras just as much focused on him as the actual game when he was filmed dancing with random women, posing for selfies with fans, and stretching his arms wide like Christ. He celebrated more wildly than any fan could possibly do, when Marcos Rojo scored the goal that took Argentina into the knockout rounds, and not content with his celebrations, he also gave opposition fans the finger. That all might not have gone down well with FIFA, but the fans lapped it up. Unfortunately, he was also seen slumped in his seat and was taken to hospital after one game for medical checks after deep concerns about his health and welfare.

Maradona was at the 2018 World Cup purely as a fan, but back in 2010 he was carrying the hopes of the nation as their manager. It was a pretty disastrous two-year tenure but threw up some brilliant moments; Maradona sliding on his belly across the rain-sodden turf while celebrating a dramatic late goal Martin Palermo scored against Peru to move them closer to qualifying for the finals, Maradona ordered those on the losing side during a training game to line up in the goalmouth and lower their trousers so the winners could take pot shots at their bare backsides.

During the tournament, when asked by a journalist whether his players were allowed to have sex, Maradona gave the memorable reply: 'Of course, as long as the women do all the work! Then there was his parting shot to journalists after Argentina's elimination from the World Cup finals following a 4-0 thrashing by Germany, in which he told them to 'suck his d★★★' during an extraordinary rant.

Everyone who loves and follows football passionately will have their own opinion on who was the greatest - Maradona or Pelé. While Maradona is often painted as the villain, Pelé is the hero, with a far less inappropriate life off the field, and even on it. Although, it must be said that Pelé had his moments!

There was a falling out between the two giants of the world game, which lasted for many years, which was sparked when Maradona made some sordid unsubstantiated allegations about his rival. He claimed in the late 1990s that Pelé had a gay relationship with one of his youth coaches at Santos. In my best selling book *Pelé: His Life and Times,* the close friend of the Brazilian, Celso Grellet, told me that Pelé wanted to respond to the allegations but decided to keep his opinions to himself. In the book, Grellet is quoted as saying: "Maradona had said that Pelé had had a homosexual experience. It was never true, but Pelé is a big man and decided he would not respond. Pelé is heavily involved in the anti-drugs campaign, particularly the abuse of drugs in sport, and Maradona was clearly an ill man.'

In his 2000 autobiography, Maradona accused Pelé of letting his former team-mate Garrincha 'die in misery', adding 'I'd like to see him fight the rich and powerful that are damaging football.'

However, they eventually healed the long running rift. They

embraced in public during an event in Paris in 2016, not long after Pelé had undergone hip surgery. "It is really nice to see him like this, healthy, and being able to join us," Maradona said, "we should hang together always. And enough of the fighting, enough of the barbs between us."

Pelé agreed, saying "this is a moment of peace" and he was one of the first to pay tribute to Maradona after his passing. He wrote on Instagram: "I have lost a dear friend and the world has lost a legend… One day I hope we will play soccer together in the sky."

THE LEGEND, MYTHS, FALL OUTS

While Diego Maradona earned millions during his glittering career, he lost much of this over the years due to tax cases with Italian authorities in which he paid out millions. In 2016, he told the Italian newspaper *Corriere della Serra* that he had made all outstanding tax bill payments. However, it has been claimed he had a remaining sum of £33million to pay to Italian authorities which put his net worth at a mere £100,000.

Diego emerged from an impoverished background to escape the slums of a provincial town. He was given a ball soon after he could run. "I was three years old and I slept hugging that ball all night," he said. He made his debut in 1976, playing for Argentinos Juniors when he was just 15-years-old. He started to build his reputation as one of the best youngsters ever to emerge from South America, scoring 115 goals in 167 appearances.

In 1981, he moved to Boca Juniors for £3 million. After playing with the club for a year, Diego transferred clubs again moving to Barcelona for £5million, a then world record fee.

During his career, he played for Argentina in four World Cups, captain in the 1986 World Cup in Mexico where he led the team to victory. He scored 34 goals and earned 91 caps.

He worked as a manager with teams including Argentina, Al-Wasl, Fujairah and Dorados. Most recently, Diego was the manager of Gimnasia, a role he took on in September 2019.

His place in football's pantheon is not in doubt but Argentina's favourite son battled alcohol, drug addiction and obesity. He left behind a complicated personal and familial legacy.

Born to a devout Catholic family, Maradona grew up in Villa Fiorito, a shanty town south of capital Buenos Aries. Life was tough in an area tourists were well advised to avoid. Football was the chance of his big escape. His father, affectionately known as Don Diego, was a factory worker who once refused to let his son attend trials for Argentinos Juniors because there was not enough money in the sport. His mother, Dona Tota, raised eight children - Diego was the eldest. Dona was the biggest influence and a calming presence on her street-wise son. When Dona Tota died in 2011 it was national news in Argentina, with the country's biggest newspapers and TV stations running obituaries.

Dona wanted Diego to become an accountant. In his autobiography, Diego describes how his mother would skip meals and pretend to be ill just to be able to feed her kids. When he started earning big bucks, it was his family that he looked after first.

Two of Maradona's brothers became professional footballers. Raul, known as Lalo, had a brief stint with Boca Juniors and Spanish club Granada before spending much of his career in the US. Hugo, known as El Turco, played in Spain with Rayo Vallecano and in Austria with Rapid Vienna, before becoming a cult hero with numerous clubs in Japan.

Maradona's private life was even more colourful than his career on the pitch, and that's saying something! Maradona is survived by five children - at least those known - and his former wife, 58-year-old Claudia Villafan, with whom he split in 2004 after 20 years of marriage. He was also survived by a string of mistresses, girlfriends, and former partners.

Diego met first wife Claudia Villafan, with whom I was photographed outside of the London hotel with Ossie and Diego, prior to setting off for White Lane for Ossie's testimonial match, when she was 17 and he 19. They married after a long engagement in 1989, and were married for 25 years, but it was an extremely fiery relationship. Diego had two children with Claudia, who, in her time, has been a film producer, reality TV star and actress.

Their marriage was littered with constant speculation of Diego's infidelity until they divorced in 2004, although they continued to be seen together in the years that followed, including at the 2006 World Cup. Despite drifting apart they still managed to make more headlines together in 2018, when Maradona sued Claudia for allegedly stealing his money and using it to buy apartments in Florida.

While two of his children, daughters Dalma and Giannina, were Claudia's, Diego has at least three other offspring with unconfirmed rumours of many more.

In 2016, after nearly 30 years of denying paternity, Diego finally recognised Diego Jr Sinagra as his son. He had been born in September 1986 after Diego's affair with model Cristina Sinagra while he played for Napoli. Despite years of campaigning from his mum – and even rumours that the Pope had got involved – Diego refused to accept he was the father, despite an Italian court proclaiming him as the father as early as 1995. He finally had a change of heart after another love child, Jana, got to know him by secretly meeting with him at a gym he attended in Buenos Aires. Maradona fathered Jana, now a lingerie model, after a brief fling with nightclub worker Valeria Sabalain while still married to Claudia.

Diego Jr played in the lower leagues in Italy, and publicly posed for pictures with Diego after a family reunion. Diego said: "I'm very happy because I've been reunited with my son. I've been reunited with him as I was reunited with Jana. I love him a lot and he's very like me."

More women came forward with paternity claims against Maradona. In March 2019, he accepted paternity of three Cuban children, from two mothers, although their identities remain a secret. But circumstantial evidence pointed to Diego as the father, as he had spent many months in Havana between 2000 and 2005 while undergoing treatment for a cocaine habit, befriending then-President Fidel Castro. Maradona got a tattoo of Castro's face on his leg.

At least three other women have come forward claiming Maradona to be the father of their children, but he did not publicly confirm they were his before his death.

His youngest child, Diego Fernando, is seven, born in 2013. Maradona had been dating his mother, Veronica Ojeda, before dumping her when she was four months pregnant for Rocio

Oliva, 30 years his junior.

Much closer to home was Diego's relationship with Manchester City and Argentinian goalscoring legend Sergio Agüero. Agüero was married to Maradona's daughter, Giannina, for four years from 2009 to 2013. Agüero was there at the birth of the couple's son Benjamin in 2009. The couple separated in 2012. Not long after separating from Diego's daughter, their relationship fell apart in acrimonious fashion with Maradona branding Sergio - the father of his grandson Benjamin - "a wimp".

On Diego's premature death, his lawyer shared an image of Maradona from his home in 2018; it was spotted on social media a picture of Agüero hanging on the wall... Agüero's face had been completely blacked out by Maradona. Clearly, their relationship had not been healed!

Yet, Sergio penned a poignant message following the death of his former father-in-law. After his involvement for Manchester City against Olympiakos, Agüero wrote: "We are never going to forget you. You will always be with us. #GraciasDiego RIP."

After splitting from Veronica Ojeda, Maradona got together with Rocio Oliva, who at the time was just 23, 30 years his junior. Rocio was a former professional footballer herself. With his footballing skills and her relationship with Diego, Rocio become a celebrity in Argentina. They were engaged 18 months after they met. But they never married and split up in 2018 after a series of blazing rows, the biggest was when she refused to follow him to Mexico after he got the job as Dorados manager.

When Maradona was hospitalised and then needed surgery on his brain, a distraught Rocio blamed alcohol addiction as the cause. She said: "On September 9 he was admitted for the same reason but this time round he was in a worse condition than before. What's happening here is simple. You can keep him in hospital three or four days and get him better by hydrating him and giving him vitamins but that's not the solution. Diego takes sleeping pills, but Diego's problem is alcohol and it's well known. Diego is still drinking and whoever says he isn't is a liar. He needs to be treated for his alcohol addiction."

Diego's drinking binges, womanising, obesity, and drug dependency are as legendary as his footballing glories, trophies and World Cup triumphs. Former Oasis front man Liam Gallagher recalled in 2017 how Maradona threatened to have him shot when they met in a bar following a gig in Argentina. The Gallagher brothers were sat in a bar when Maradona and a 30-strong entourage burst through the doors and Liam asked if he could go upstairs and meet the great man. 'He's gone upstairs with a load of f***ing madheads and a load of f***ing women of the night,' Liam recalled.

'We steamed up there and there's loads of f***ing activity going on and Maradona's in the middle of the room doing football tricks with a bottle top. And his eyes were f***king like that [wide] and ours weren't far off and I just went like, "It's a bit moody in here, let's get a quick picture with him and f*** off."

'And he's sweating his b******s off and we turn around [to the interpreter] and he says: "He told me to tell you, if you leave with any of these b*****s, he'll have you shot."'

Noel Gallagher posted the picture they managed to get with Maradona after hearing the news of his death.

Maradona recorded a heartbreaking message about his 'angel' youngest son hours before his death. He asked the stepfather of his son to take good care of the seven-year-old.

Maradona shared son Dieguito Fernando with his former long-term girlfriend, Veronica Ojeda. In the recording, he told Mario Baudry, the boyfriend of his son's mother: 'Look after her and look after my angel, who is incomparable.' Veronica attended the funeral alongside Dieguito.

THE TRIBUTES

Diego Maradona's sudden death at the age of 60 led to an outpouring of testimonials, tributes, a wealth of emotions from every big name in world football. Lionel Messi joined the thousands of current and former footballers who paid their own special tributes to football icon Diego Maradona. Maradona's death led to floods of tributes from the footballing world, including Pelé, Cristiano Ronaldo, Gary Lineker and Paul Gascoigne in memory of the legendary Argentine figure.

Messi, whose magical football career has been likened to that of Maradona, delivered his tribute: "A very sad day for all Argentines and for football," he wrote on Instagram. "He leaves us but does not leave, because Diego is eternal. I keep all the beautiful moments lived with him and I wanted to take the opportunity to send my condolences to all his family and friends. RIP". Maradona and Messi are two of the greatest footballers of all time and back in 2005 the pair shared the pitch together. In 2005 Messi was an 18-years-old but had already helped Barcelona to win La Liga, making seven appearances in the league title victory, starting to show his brilliance and was, like many before him, being compared to Maradona. The teenager linked up with a 45-year-old Maradona for an Argentina All Stars team in a charity match along with Sergio Agüero, Diego Simeone and Juan Sebastian Veron. The link up play between the two No 10s really caught the attention. From the highlights, the two men were on the same wavelength with passes, one-twos, and flicks. They played other charity matches together, the most recent in 2016.

They were together again when Maradona took on the job as Argentina manager between 2008 and 2010. Martin Palermo's injury time penalty in Argentina's penultimate game of the 2010 World Cup qualifying against Peru, followed by Mario Bolatti's 84th minute winner to take Maradona's Argentina into the finals in South Africa where they breezed through their group before beating Mexico 3-1 in the second round. However in the quarters they were embarrassed by a 4-0 win for Germany and Maradona was soon sacked.

Born a year after Maradona's heroics at the 1986 World Cup, he grew up though watching Maradona's rise to global sensation at Napoli as the legendary figure broke down barriers in Italy. Current Argentina captain Lionel Messi admitted five years ago that Maradona helped shape his path into football. "I never followed anyone in particular, although when I started to think for myself Diego had recently returned home," he said in 2015. "That was in 1993. He joined Newell's Old Boys when he came back from Spain and was part of the national team that qualified for USA '94. If anybody inspired me starting out, it was undoubtedly him." They shared a close bond as Messi's career began to take shape in 2005, linking up with the national team in 2008 when Maradona became head coach.

Messi later paid his special public tribute to the late Maradona after scoring in Barcelona's 4-0 La Liga win over Osasuna. Messi, 33, unveiled a Newell's Old Boys shirt - one of Argentina great Maradona's former clubs - after his side's fourth goal.

The Argentine looked to the screen showing Maradona's picture at the Nou Camp and raised both hands in the air. Messi was also on the books of Argentine team Newell's Old Boys as a youngster before joining Barcelona. Maradona's playing career included Barca. Messi spent six years there as a youngster before joining Barcelona's famed La Masia youth academy. Messi has previously spoken about his memories of watching Maradona play for Newell's, telling TyC Sports in 2013 that he was in the stadium for Maradona's debut in 1993. "I don't remember much, I was very young, but I saw Maradona on the pitch the day he made his debut against Emelec," Messi said. Maradona scored his only goal for Newell's that day and Messi imitated his celebration after scoring against Osasuna, later posting a side-by-side image on Instagram of himself and Maradona.

Now after scoring, Messi lifted his shirt to reveal a red and black replica kit of his hometown club. It was a number 10 shirt, which Maradona wore during his brief spell at the Rosario side in 1993. Barca had paid tribute before kick-off hanging a framed, signed shirt of his above the presidential box. Players held a minute's silence in front of an old Barcelona shirt bearing the number 10. It was an emotional tribute from the 33-year-old but he was booked by the referee for removing his shirt.

Barcelona faced a fine of up to 3,000 Euros in accordance with article 91 of the RFEF Disciplinary Code. The article reads: "The footballer who, on the occasion of having scored a goal or for any cause derived from the vicissitudes of the game, raises his shirt and displays any kind of advertising, slogan, legend, acronyms, anagrams or drawings, whatever their content or the purpose of the action, will be punished, as the author of a serious offence, with a fine of up to 3,000 Euros and a warning." The club would pay the fine to RFEF at the end of the season. Barcelona boss Ronald Koeman called Messi's tribute a "great moment in every way" after the game, saying: "It was a great moment. First, for the goal that Leo scored and then for the gesture he had for the death of Diego Maradona. He had surely been thinking of what he would do. For me, it was a great moment in every way.

On the constant debate whether Messi is as good, or better, than his fellow countryman, the Barca star once said, "Even if I played for a million years, I'd never come close to Maradona. Not that I'd want to anyway. He's the greatest there's ever been."

Maradona's former clubs and the Argentina national team's Twitter account were among the first to pay tribute to him. Barcelona, where he enjoyed two seasons between 1982 and 1984, tweeted: 'Thank you for everything, Diego'.

Boca Juniors, where Maradona began and ended his career in Argentina, tweeted: 'Eternal thank you. Eternal Diego.'

Napoli, where Maradona spent seven years between 1984 and 1991 and won the club's only two Serie A titles in 1987 and 1990, wrote: 'Always in our hearts. Ciao Diego'.

They then tweeted again, saying: 'The world awaits our words but there are no words to describe the pain we're going through. Now is the time to grieve'.

Manchester United striker Marcus Rashford joined tributes with just one word, 'Legendary', alongside a picture of the former Napoli and Barcelona icon in his heyday.

Cristiano Ronaldo posted an old picture of himself with Maradona on his Instagram account and wrote: 'Today I say goodbye to a friend and the world says goodbye to an eternal genius. One of the best ever. An unparalleled magician. He leaves too soon, but leaves a legacy without limits and a void that will never be filled. Rest in peace, ace. You will never be forgotten.'

Former Argentina coach Marcelo Bielsa said the nation has lost an "idol". Bielsa was now coach of Leeds United. He struggled to process the loss of his compatriot and national hero, like all Argentines. "He was for us, and will continue to be, an idol," said Bielsa, who managed Argentina from 1998 to 2004. "Given the fact he is not with us any more brings great sadness. We have lost an idol and it makes us feel weak. What really stood out was his relationship with the public. Everything he did as a footballer was of a beauty which cannot be matched. Maradona was an artist. Players with such individual brilliance, they don't know what it is to play with pressure. In terms of what he signifies to us, Diego made us live the fantasy that an idol makes you feel. The myth that is that person makes us belief that what he does, we can all do. That's why the loss of an idol always hurts the people who are excluded the most. They are the ones who most need someone to show them that they can triumph."

Bielsa worked with Maradona once when he managed him in an Argentina XI against a Rest of the World side for his testimonial 19 years ago at Boca Juniors' La Bombonera stadium, Maradona's last before retiring. Bielsa will never forget the adoration and love the people showed him. "In that game what really stood out was his relationship with the public. But then everything he did as a footballer was a beauty, which cannot be matched."

Bielsa remembers his second goal against England in the 1986

World Cup quarter-final, a thing of beauty, like a cathedral or work of art. "To describe something as a work of art is something you can't put to too many things. For me that goal was similar to the impression you get when you see an architectural work of art, where you are astounded. For example, when you see a beautiful church, you are taken aback and that is what it was like for me when Diego scored. Diego was an artist and his art received infinite recognition.

"What makes me really sad is that people like Maradona and Messi, who showed their individual brilliance through dribbling, they are versions of players that stop repeating themselves," he said. "For example, Kylian Mbappé could be said to be the best player in the world right now, but his art is not comparable to that of Maradona's."

Jürgen Klopp says meeting Diego was like being with the Pope. The hugely successful Liverpool manager and No 1 rated world coach, described the time he met Maradona and why he puts Cristiano Ronaldo and Lionel Messi are ahead of him in his personal best-ever list. "The best through my lifetime. Maybe not now, I saw Cristiano and Messi now. In my career, he was the standout player. His life shows how nice it can be when you're world-class and how difficult it can be too. An impressive figure. I met him once which for a player of my level was like meeting the Pope. You can see reactions all over the world. If we showed him the respect he deserves while alive instead of selfies, we could have helped him."

Former Manchester United defender Rio Ferdinand posted a series of pictures of him with Maradona over the years, and wrote a heartfelt message: 'My 1st football hero. Few people have impact over generations like this man did. The greatest, the best, the artist, the man...charismatic, a leader...A WINNER! One of the main reasons why I went out on my estate to kick a ball, pretending to be Diego. RIP Diego Armando Maradona.'

The England national team's Twitter account, on the wrong end of Maradona's magic and infamous handball 34 years ago, wrote: 'Unforgettable. Farewell, Diego. A legend of our game.'

Sky Sports pundit Jamie Carragher tweeted: 'I'll never forget watching Diego Maradona as an 8 yr old at the World Cup in Mexico. Never seen anything like it on that stage since. Sad news #Maradona'.

Former England and Liverpool striker Michael Owen added: 'Quite simply - a player like no other. Rest In Peace Diego Maradona.'

AC Milan striker Zlatan Ibrahimovic posted a picture of himself laughing with Maradona on Instagram: 'Maradona is not dead he is immortal. God gave the world the best gifted football player of all times. He will live forever and ever.'

England captain Harry Kane tweeted a picture of when he met Maradona in the Tottenham dressing room in 2017, and wrote: 'Privileged to have met him. Very sad news. RIP Diego Maradona.'

Jose Mourinho took to his Instagram account to share a picture of him on the bench with Maradona, and wrote: 'Don Diego. F★★k friend I miss you'. Mourinho revealed that Diego used to call him after he suffered a big defeat, but never after the ex-Real Madrid coach won a game. I know him well enough and in my big defeats, he would always call me. In my big victories, never. But I will miss Diego, and I am very sad but I have a smile because with him, every minute I spent with him was to laugh.'

Mourinho added: 'There is Maradona and there is Diego. Maradona I don't need to speak about because the world knows and nobody will forget. Diego is different, the people that are the big friends of him, the people that share dressing rooms with him, colleagues, these guys are privileged. I can say he was a good friend of mine, but my contacts with him were by telephone and we met of course a few times. He had a big, big, big, big heart. That's the guy I miss, because his football we can find every time we miss him, if we Google we will find it. But Diego, no. I know him well enough and in my big defeats, he would always call me. In my big victories, never. Then there's Diego the guy. That one, I miss. I feel sorry that I didn't spend more time with him, I would have loved to. I think his family, his friends and colleagues are very privileged to know him well and spend time with him. But I will miss Diego, and I am very sad but I have a smile because with him, every minute I spent with him was to laugh."

Spanish outlet *Marca* released a video that demonstrated the respect between the two. The footage shows Maradona and Mourinho speaking in Spanish in 2010 at Madrid's training ground while Mourinho was in charge of Los Blancos. They are sitting in the dugout, and conversation turns to Maradona's playing days. He can be heard saying: "I tried my hardest, busting my a★★★, and when I passed it to my teammate they would often miss the target." Mourinho responds by joking: "The thing is, to play in a team you know that if you shoot, you score. Another thing is to pass to a teammate, and you don't know if they will (score)." They burst into laughter, and later in the interview they embrace each other in a big hug, with Mourinho kissing Maradona on the cheek. Mourinho says: "Thanks for the visit. A kiss for your family," while Maradona replies: "I love you and I respect you a lot."

Pep Guardiola paid tribute to Maradona describing him as one of the 'few incredible players' in football history. 'First (I think about) Sergio. His son, Diego was his grandfather. There was a banner in Argentina which says, "It doesn't matter what you have done in your life, it matters what you have done in our lives." Imagine what Maradona would have done in our generation (of football). There are few incredible players in our history, he's one of them. He was someone who made this sport better. On behalf of Manchester City a big hug for all his family.' Guardiola said of Agüero: 'It's difficult for me to talk about his feelings. The game against Olympiakos was hard. Especially for his son, it's tough. He knew Maradona well and his son, it's his grandfather. It's a sad situation for his family, but he's OK.'

Former England captain David Beckham, who was involved in controversy during a clash with Argentina at the 1998 World

Cup, posted a picture of himself with his arm around Maradona to Instagram and wrote: 'A sad day for Argentina and a sad day for football as we celebrate the greatness of what this man gave us... Someone that played with passion, spirit and was nothing less than a pure genius.. I was so excited to meet Diego and we will all miss him. Rest In Peace.'

Tottenham and Argentina forward Erik Lamela posted an image of himself with Maradona and Sergio Agüero and pictures of his hero in action and lifting the World Cup. Lamela wrote: 'For me you are eternal... dear D1EG0!'

Chelsea midfielder Jorginho, who used to play for Maradona's former club Napoli, shared a photo of himself with the Argentine legend, adding the hashtags 'maestro', 'respect' and 'goodbye great'.

Chelsea and Germany striker Timo Werner posted an image of him shaking hands with Maradona on international duty with the caption: 'Rest in peace, legend.'

Stan Collymore tweeted: 'The football Gods shone brightly on this one. What an incredible, incredible footballer.' Everton striker Richarlison tweeted a picture of Maradona in a Brazil shirt, with just a sad face emoji to accompany it.

At the Argentinian embassy in London, fans left flowers and pictures of Maradona while a banner outside said 'Thank you, Diego' with a picture of him lifting the World Cup. cross all Premier League games that weekend, the players took part in a minute of applause for Diego. Carlo Ancelotti was in tears as Maradona was remembered before Everton's game with Leeds United. Sky Sports cameras panned in on a visibly emotional Ancelotti. Tears were in the Italian's eyes. Ancelotti paid his own tribute before the game, saying: "He was very humble and it is a big loss for football, but the memories will always be there. He was a fantastic player who helped football around the world. At this time he was the best player in the world, and the best player I ever played against. He was so difficult to stop and had unbelievable quality. He never complained on the pitch. I tried to stop him with strong contact but he never complained and after that we became good friends. We met at events after our playing careers were finished and it was always good to spend time with him. He was not only a footballer but a great example to show everywhere. But this is the life. I will always keep fantastic memories of him. You have to explain Maradona by what he did and I think that World Cup, and I was there in '86 but I never played, he practically won it alone. Of course Argentina had fantastic players in their team like Burruchaga and Valdano but Maradona practically won that World Cup alone."

Front pages from across the globe paid tribute to the sporting legend, a day after he passed away. From Europe to the USA, India to Malaysia, Nigeria and throughout South America, photos of Maradona's face were across newspaper pages both front and back. In his native Argentina, tributes ran from a simple 'thank you, champion' to 'I don't want this pain in my heart'.

Clarin, Argentina's best-selling newspaper, led with the famous picture of Maradona holding the Jules Rimet trophy aloft after the 1986 World Cup final with the headline: 'There won't be another like him'. They had been the first to report Maradona's death from heart failure. "And one day it happened,' read their obituary. 'The sentence that was written various times but which destiny dribbled past is now part of a sad reality: Diego Armando Maradona is dead.' But, said the paper: 'Maradona is in the present, even though you have to write about those who have died in the past tense.' The obituary finished with the unique interview Maradona gave himself on an Argentine TV show in 2005 when he asked himself what he'd say at his funeral. 'Thanks for having played football, because it's the sport that gave me the most happiness, the most freedom, it's like touching the sky with your hands.

'Thanks to the ball. Yes, I'd put up a tombstone that said: "Thanks to the ball."'

La Nacion's front page showed Argentina's World Cup hero balancing the ball on his head with the message: 'Thank you, champion.'

'An emotional goodbye across the world for a footballer

for all time,' it read. 'A phenomenon who combined talent and leadership on the pitch and reached unlimited popularity.' It also carried news of Maradona's farewell at the presidential palace, the Casa Rosada, where his body will lie in state for three days starting on Thursday – only the second non-president to receive the honour after Formula 1 champion Juan Manuel Fangio. Their obituary described Maradona's death as 'the news that left the country in total shock'.

La Nacion's illustrators all paid tribute to Argentina's biggest symbol, with Nik Gaturro imagining Maradona's meeting with God. 'Well, now I can retire,' he says, leaving a throne with Maradona's famous 10 on it vacant for El Diego. While both newspapers carried Maradona's date of birth and death on their front page, Argentina's leading sports newspaper Ole went with '1960 – Infinity' instead alongside El Diez kissing the World Cup trophy. It was no surprise to see so many papers leading off the World Cup triumph, Maradona's finest moment for Argentina that cemented him in the hearts of the entire nation.

Cronica turned it round, however, with their front page showing Maradona standing on the World Cup and the headline AD10S – playing on the shirt number he made his own in Mexico in 1986. The Buenos Aires tabloid detailed what Argentines were feeling: 'Hurt, stupor, incredulousness, tears, emotion, gratefulness, adoration.' They described him as 'the small giant who gave us so much sporting joy over the course of his career' who 'always lived between heaven and hell, without shades of grey or nuances'. Cronica, one of the main papers in Buenos Aires, where he lived, ran a superlative tribute which ended with the words: 'Thank you for everything, champion.'

Pagina 12 went with an even more emotive cover which captured the general feeling in Argentina, overlaying an image of Maradona in the blue-and-white of Argentina looking up to the sky with the headline: 'I don't want this sorrow in my heart.' As their lead writer put it: 'He is not in History, he made History. He wrote it with a ball stuck to his left foot. 'Few images sum up

Argentina like the one of Diego lifting the World Cup in 1986. Few represent so well what we wanted to be and what we once were.'

Italian papers mainly lead with pictures of him in the blue and white shirt of his country, despite his many years playing in the country for Napoli. *La Gazzetta dello Sport*, with a picture of Maradona kissing the iconic World Cup trophy in 86, say: 'I saw Maradona'. Tuttosport have the picture of him being carried on the shoulders of his team-mates in the immediate aftermath of his World Cup triumph at the Aztec stadium, with the headline: 'AD10S', referencing the No 10 shirt that became synonymous with his career. *Corrierre dello Sport* have a picture of Maradona in his Napoli days under the headline 'Diego Lives'.

Spanish papers also ran glowing tributes, though many featured him in his Barcelona strip as opposed to the colours of his country. El Periodico printed an image of Maradona in a Barcelona shirt along with the caption 'Adios', but styled so that it could also read: 'A God' *Mundo Deportivo* – the Barcelona based publication – also run with an 'AD10S' style headline and say all of sport, not just football, is mourning his death. AS's front page read 'D10S Ha Muerto' with a picture of Maradona wearing an Argentina shirt while stood in front of the sun. Sport use the same picture as *Tuttosport* in Italy but with the headline: 'God is already in heaven.' *Marca* newspaper also ran with a touching quote of Maradona's which read: 'If I am reborn, I want to be a footballer. And I want to be Diego Armando Maradona again. I am a player who has made people happy, and that is enough for me.'

'God is dead,' declared France's *L'Equipe* – far from the only publication to compare the 5ft 4ins Argentine to the Almighty. Newspapers in Denmark, Sweden, Germany, the UK and Ireland also made space for Maradona on their front and back pages, admiring his talents. Two newspaper in Nigeria also found space for Maradona, such was his international fame, while his passing was also noted in some Middle Eastern titles. His footballing genius was also translated in Malaysian and Hindi, showing how truly international an icon he was.

THREE DAYS OF NATIONAL MOURNING

Diego Maradona has always held legendary status in Argentina and his death proved just how much he was revered in his homeland. His death triggered global mourning, but it was felt most passionately in a country that regarded him as a national hero. Fans in Argentina refer to him as 'El Dios', 'The God', but is also a play on words on his number 10 shirt, 'El Diez'.

Argentina's president Alberto Fernandez announced three days of national mourning as he paid tribute on social media, tweeting: "You took us to the highest point of the world, and made us immensely happy. You were the greatest of all. Thank you for having been with us, Diego. We will miss you all our lives."

The Argentinean Football Federation issued a tribute: "The Argentine Football Association, through its President Claudio Tapia, expresses its deepest sorrow for the death of our legend, Diego Armando Maradona. You will always be in our hearts."

Thousands of fans paid their final respects at the presidential palace in Buenos Aires. Some wept, some clapped, others blew kisses and said prayers as they filed past the coffin displayed at the Casa Rosada. A million people visited his casket.

Maradona's coffin was draped in Argentina's national flag and football shirt, bearing his trademark number 10 on the back.

There were tense scenes when the Casa Rosada opened its doors, as some fans pushed and shoved against the barriers, which were lined with security forces. By mid-afternoon queues stretched back for more than a kilometre, and police clashed with mourners as they tried to close off the palace in anticipation of the wake. There were reports of tear gas and rubber bullets being used as officers in riot gear struggled to hold back the crowd. One well-wisher, Rubén Hernández, thought the police had overreacted. "We were calm lining up and suddenly, the police started to fire rubber bullets," he said, quoted by Reuters news agency. "Crazy, I just want to say goodbye to Diego." Authorities were eventually forced to stop public viewing of the coffin to keep the peace.

Katy Watson, the BBC's South American correspondent, reported, "The atmosphere varied greatly outside the presidential palace. Those waiting to go in were singing and chanting. 'If you don't jump, you're English,' is one of the favourite chants of Argentinians about the 1986 match with England and *that* goal – the Hand of God – something many here saw as a sort of payback after the Falklands War, known here as the Malvinas. But on the other side of the square, there was another line with those coming out, many wiping away tears or hugging each other after processing what had happened. This wasn't just the death of Argentina's superstar footballer, but the passing of a man that many saw as a national icon, a star who made Argentina famous – and most of all, a very human role-model who Argentinians loved, flaws and all. A man who was respected for achieving so much, yet never forgetting his roots."

His family and former teammates had taken part in a private ceremony earlier in the day. Maradona was then buried in a private ceremony after a day of emotional scenes in Buenos Aires. Two dozen relatives and close friends attended the final ceremony. The motorised funeral cortege drove his body to the Bella Vista cemetery on the outskirts of the city, where he was buried next to the graves of his parents.

"His unparalleled footballing skill transformed him into one of the best-known people in the world, crossing frontiers and being universally recognised as the world's best player," said the official mourning decree. He was someone who touched the sky with his hands but never took his feet off the ground," said Argentine president Alberto Fernandez.

A post-mortem confirmed that Maradona had suffered heart failure, which caused a pulmonary edema. It's stated that dilated cardiomyopathy, a medical condition in which the heart muscle becomes weakened and enlarged and cannot pump enough blood to the rest of the body, was also detected.

Maradona's former lawyer and long-time friend, Matias Morla, demanded an investigations into his death, alleging "criminal idiocy" that lead to the football icon's death. In tribute, he also added: "To define Diego in this moment of deep desolation and pain I can say: he was a good son, he was the best soccer player in history and he was an honest person. Rest in peace, brother."

Morla claimed Maradona was left for 12 hours without aid at some point before his death, 'It is inexplicable that for 12 hours my friend had no attention or check-up from the personnel dedicated to these ends,' he said in a statement. Morla claimed it was 'criminal idiocy' that an ambulance took 30 minutes to arrive and vowed that the circumstances surrounding Maradona's death would be 'investigated to the end'.

Maradona's personal physician was forced to apologise prior to his death after his family were furious with what he claimed to be the final publicly released photo of him alive. Diego was recovering after undergoing emergency surgery to remove a subdural haematoma, an accumulation of blood between a membrane and his brain. After responding well to the surgery, he was cleared to be discharged to his home by his doctor, Dr Luque, who shared a picture of them. Maradona was seen smiling alongside Luque in a picture which was promptly circulated as the final picture of Maradona alive. According to *Clarin*, his family were unhappy with Luque with the release of the picture. Prior to Diego's death, the doctor apologised for any upset caused but insisted he had permission from Maradona to share the picture. "I thought it was an image that would erase the other, that Diego had left the day of the match against Patronato. Because it really is fantastic now," said Luque at the time, "I thought that this photo was going to have a very good acceptance from everyone, but it was not so. So I offer my apologies to those who felt offended, criticised or believed that the photo was not appropriate. Secondly, the photo was agreed with Diego. I want to clarify that it was not my decision. It was not something that I decided on my own."

In Diego's final interview to Argentinian newspaper *Clarin* days earlier, that prior to his return to football as Gimnasia manager sometimes wondered "if people will still love me." But he "felt that love with people is never going to end." He said: "I am going to be eternally grateful to the people. Every day they surprise me, what I experienced in this return to Argentine football I will never forget. It exceeded what I could imagine. Because I was out for a long time and sometimes I wonder if people will still love me, if they will continue to feel the same. When I entered the field in Gimnasia on the day of the presentation I felt that love with people is never going to end."

Asked if he had any regrets from his life, he said: "I went and I am very happy. Soccer gave me everything I have, more than I ever imagined. And if I hadn't had that addiction, I could have played a lot more. But today that is past, I am fine and what I regret the most is not having my parents. I always make that wish, one more day with Tota but I know that from heaven she is proud of me and that she was very happy."

Asked his wish for Argentina, he added: "My wish is that this pandemic passes as soon as possible and that my Argentina can move forward. I want all Argentines to be well, we have a beautiful country and I trust that our President will be able to get us out of this moment. It makes me very sad when I see children who do not have enough to eat, I know what it is to go hungry, I know what it feels like to feel when you do not eat for several days and that cannot happen in my country. That is my wish, to see the Argentines happy, with work and eating every day."

Boca Juniors and Newell's Old Boys paid tribute to him before their game on Sunday. Argentina legend Maradona played for both clubs, winning a title with Boca in 1981. Both sets of players wore special shirts for a minute's applause around a flag of the 1986 World Cup winner. Maradona banners were all over the stadium but the most emotional moment came after Edwin Cardona scored his first of two goals on a night Boca won 2-0. After scoring a free-kick the Boca players went over to Maradona's daughter Dalma, who was sat in the stands and applauded her. She was overcome with emotion, crying in her father's box at the Bombonera. Both sets of players had Maradona's name on their shirts. The referee had 'Gracias Diego' on the back of his shirt.

The Copa Diego Armando Maradona is the new name for the Argentine League Cup, which is a replacement for the league this season. As with all other Serie A matches, it was preceded by a minute's silence. The game stopped in the tenth minute for a round of applause. Napoli also wore a special kit of light blue-and-white-striped shirts reminiscent of Argentina's strip. Club captain Lorenzo Insigne laid a bouquet of flowers under a photo of Maradona before the match, and he marked his goal during by collecting and kissing a shirt with Maradona's name on it. After scoring in their 4-0 win on Saturday against Osasuna, Lionel Messi celebrated by wearing Maradona's Newell's Old Boys shirt and pointing to the heavens.

Maradona remained a lifelong supporter of Boca and often cut a crazed figure as he watched games from his box on the halfway line at the ground. Maradona enjoyed two spells at his boyhood club, from 1981 to 1982 and again between 1995 and 1997. He won just one major honour in his time there – the Argentine Primera Division in 1981. In his first spell he scored 28 times in 40 appearances, earning a move to Europe and Barcelona, where his career was catapulted further into the spotlight.

Boca paid immediate tribute to Maradona on Wednesday night as news of his passing broke, tweeting a picture of the former great in the famous blue and yellow strip with the words: 'Eternal thanks. Eternal Diego.' Their Copa Libertadores clash with Brazilian side Internacional was called off just hours after Maradona's death after the Argentine club asked for permission for it to be postponed. Boca fans poured onto the streets of Buenos Aires and gathered outside the famous Bombonera stadium to remember their idol.

POLICE INVESTIGATE MANSLAUGHTER

In line with his chaotic life, the aftermath of Diego Maradona's death proved controversial. Within days police searched the house and private clinic of Lorenzo Luque, Maradona's doctor. They were trying to establish if there was negligence or even possible manslaughter in his treatment. Maradona's daughters demanded to know what medication their father was on. Thirty police officers raided 39-year-old Dr Luque's house four days after his death, with another 20 going into his clinic in the capital Buenos Aires. Dr Luque had not been charged and denied any wrongdoing. Maradona had a successful operation on a brain blood clot earlier in November and had been due to be treated for alcohol dependency. The raids were ordered by prosecutors trying to build a picture of Maradona's last days at home. They retrieved computers, mobile phones and medical notes. There were suspicions that the star's convalescence at home might not have met the conditions of his discharge from the clinic, such as a 24-hour team of nurses "specialised in substance abuse", the on-call presence of doctors and a stand-by ambulance equipped with a defibrillator. Officials wanted to know about Dr Luque's involvement in Maradona's recovery arrangements at the late star's house.

In an emotional press conference Dr Luque, described as the footballer's personal physician, cried, saying he had done all he could to save the life of a friend. He said Maradona had been very sad lately. The doctor hit back at reporters: "You want to know what I am responsible for? For having loved him, for having taken care of him, for having extended his life, for having improved it to the end." The doctor said he had done "everything he could, up to the impossible". Addressing the concerns authorities were looking into, Dr Luque cast doubt on what his role actually was. "If you ask me, I'm a neurosurgeon and my job ended. I was done with him," he said referring to November's surgery - and insisting Maradona's convalescence at home was not his responsibility. "He

[Maradona] should have gone to a rehabilitation centre. He didn't want to," Dr Luque said, calling the late star "unmanageable". He did not know why there was no defibrillator or who was responsible for the fact that there was no ambulance outside Maradona's house. He added: Diego "was very sad, he wanted to be alone, and it's not because he didn't love his daughters, his family, or those around him".

The mystery over his death continued with media speculation that Maradona fell over and hit his head a week before he died but was never taken to the hospital despite suffering an injury. Italian newspaper *La Republica* claim that Maradona was not taken for a scan after falling and hitting his head at home. A lawyer representing a nurse who worked for Maradona is reported to have said: "Maradona fell to the ground seven days before his death. He fell and hit his head but they didn't take him to the hospital for an MRI or a CT scan." The same report confirmed speculation from media in Argentina that Maradona was alone in his house in Buenos Aires when he died from a heart attack. According to a preliminary autopsy report, Maradona died from 'acute lung edema and chronic heart failure'. He died in his sleep while he was resting at home. The same nurse's lawyer said that she had spoken with Maradona on the Friday before his death but was fired on the Saturday. She remained at the request of Maradona's entourage to administer his medication but was no longer taking his blood pressure or controlling him, according to her lawyer.

Maradona's daughters Dalma and Giannina gave statements questioning whether the medication their father was receiving was appropriate. *Republica* also reported that documents emerged showing that Dr Cosachov had requested 24-hour specialist and nursing assistance for Maradona before his death but Luque had not arranged for that to happen. But Luque made an emotional defence when under investigation for involuntary manslaughter - and insisted that Maradona was 'unmanageable' and should have been sent to rehab. He said: 'I was shocked when police turned up at my door. I'm going to co-operate fully. I know what I did and what I did was for Diego's benefit until the last moment. I did the best I could. I feel terrible because a friend died. I don't blame myself for anything. It's very unfair what's happening. I didn't see Diego's daughters a lot but the rest of his family, his siblings and his nephews adore me. Someone is trying to find a scapegoat here when I don't see one anywhere. We all did the best we could with Diego.'

Maradona's neurosurgeon Lorenzo Luque was quizzed on a charge of murder back in 2011. He spent two months in jail while an investigation was carried out after a neighbour was kicked to death but he was never charged.

Dr Luque received backing from Maradona's lawyer, Matias Morla, who on Twitter wrote: "I understand and comprehend the work of the prosecutors but only I know, Dr Luque, what you did for Diego's health, how you cared for him, accompanied him and how you loved him. Diego loved you and as his friend I am not going to leave you alone. You left blood, sweat and tears and the truth always wins."

Next, Argentine investigators raided the home of Maradona's psychiatrist. Prosecutors, with a judicial order, carried out searches in the house and the private office of Agustina Cosachov in Buenos Aires, as they had done with the properties of Maradona's personal doctor Lorenzo Luque. "These are routine measures when investigating the causes of death of a patient," Cosachov's lawyer, Vadim Mischanchuk, told local television. "What is being sought is a medical history on telephones and computers." Prosecutors are investigating possible "malpractice" and if necessary medical requirements for care were met, the lawyer Mischanchuk said.

Two sources close to the case, who declined to be named, told Reuters "doctors are the main ones being targeted by the prosecution" for Maradona's death. The probe was looking at possible wrongful death and medical negligence, they said.

There were reports Maradona had been prescribed a cocktail of drugs including antidepressants and antipsychotics used to treat bipolar disorder. Health experts suggested drugs could have put stress on his heart. The medications Maradona was on reportedly included Quetiapine, used to treat mood disorders including depression, schizophrenia, and bipolar disorder, and Gabapentin, used for nerve pain caused by illnesses such as diabetes but also for epilepsy. Medics detected dilated cardiomyopathy, a medical condition in which the heart muscle becomes weakened and enlarged and cannot pump enough blood to the rest of the body.

Other drugs Maradona was taking reportedly included Naltrexone, used to treat alcohol abuse; antidepressant Venlafaxine, sometimes used to treat panic attacks; Lurasidone, used to treat bipolar disorder; stomach protector Omeprazol; and a Vitamin B complex.

Discussing the medications with Argentinian news outlet *Todo Noticias*, neurology specialist Nelson Castro said: "You'd have to examine how much of each he was being given and what the criteria was, and whether he was taking them at the same time or he began with one and switched to another. There was a lot of mixing of antidepressants and antipsychotics. Several of these medicines - Quetiapine, Lurasidone, Venlafaxine - have cardiac effects and one of those is an increase in heart rate."

A lawyer to one of Maradona's nurses has also claimed he was suffering tachycardia and that his heart rate reached 115 beats per minute in the days before his death, but that the "warning signs" were ignored.

Maradona had been discharged from hospital on November 11 after a brain blood clot op and moved to a rented home on the gated estate of San Andres near Buenos Aires. The full list of his medications reportedly came from medical records now in the hands of state prosecutors. Documents including the records were seized along with phones and computers belonging to Dr Luque, a neurosurgeon by background.

Leaked WhatsApp messages published by Argentinian media showed Maradona's eldest daughter Dalma telling his psychiatrist and psychologist he needed a general GP to help coordinate his day-to-day care.

Mr Luque claimed part of the key to Maradona's care was "controlling the pills and alcohol" and he should have gone to rehab from hospital but refused.

A funeral worker was fired for taking of photo of Maradona's corpse. He was pictured taking the body to lie in state hours before he provoked the wrath of Argentina. Diego Molina received death threats for desecrating the sporting great's body after he posed for a photo with one hand resting on Maradona's head and the other giving a thumbs up. Molina was one of the men tasked with preparing Maradona's body ahead of the private open-coffin wake for family and friends. A photograph emerged of Molina standing up in a van leaving the morgue in Buenos Aires following an autopsy ahead of Maradona's body being transported to his state funeral. Since his picture was shared to social media, Molina was sent death threats from furious fans. Some called for him to be stripped of his Argentinian citizenship. Owners of the funeral parlour Sepelios Pinier confirmed to local media that the worker lost his job.

One Maradona fan who saw the picture wrote: 'I want this fat baldie who took a picture of himself by Diego's body dead. I want him dead. DEAD.' Another said: 'He should be stripped of his Argentinian citizenship. You don't do something like this. Complete lack of respect.' Maradona's lawyer Matias Morla revealed Molina's name on Twitter, along with a picture of him, as he pledged to take legal action. He wrote in a menacing message alongside his tweet: 'This is Diego Molina, the author of the photo taken beside Maradona's coffin. He's Pinier's head of burials. Diego Molina is the swine that took the picture of himself alongside Maradona. For the memory of my friend I am not going to rest until he pays for this aberration.'

It was reported that 200 police would be on guard duty at the cemetery where Maradona is buried to deter grave robbers, fearing fanatical fans will plunder his plot in a bid to collect ghoulish mementoes. The Ministry of Security said the measures would be in force for at least a week to "prevent any incident" at the Bella Vista cemetery on the outskirts of the capital. Officials feared a repeat of 1987, when the grave of former Argentina president Juan Peron was robbed.

★

The fallout over the Argentina rugby team's much-criticised tribute to Maradona extended further with some Argentines saying they will boycott the side because of what they consider an inadequate mark of respect. The Pumas used what looked like black electrical tape as armbands in their Tri-Nations test defeat to New Zealand and many Argentines felt their tribute paled in comparison to the respect shown by the All Blacks.

Before performing the traditional haka dance, the New Zealanders laid their famous black jersey with the name 'Maradona' and the number 10 on the centre spot. "People have taken note," Nery Pumpido, Argentina's goalkeeper alongside Maradona in the 1986 World Cup-winning side, told the Sol radio station. "They really got it wrong. I am never going to watch a game of theirs again."

"We know that the tribute we chose to make to Diego at the weekend caused some pain and disappointed a lot of people," captain Pablo Matera said in a recorded message alongside the whole squad. "We want everyone to know that Diego is a super important person for this team."

Spanish footballer Paula Dapena sat down and faced away when her team-mates and opponents, Deportivo Abanca, paid their respects to Maradona, three days after his death as a protest against allegations of domestic violence against him in 2014 -

no charges were brought. Dapena says she received death threats after she refused to take part in a minute's silence as a protest. The Viajes Interrias FF midfielder sat down and faced away when her team-mates and opponents, Deportivo Abanca, paid their respects. The 24-year-old told the *A Diario* radio show she had no regrets over her actions and would do it again. "I'm not willing to give a domestic abuser a minute's silence and not the victims," she said. Maradona faced accusations of domestic violence after he was caught on video in 2014 arguing with his then-girlfriend and appearing to hit her.

He denied the accusations, saying: "I grabbed the phone but I swear to God that I have never hit a woman." No charges were brought.

Dapena received lots of expressions of support "but I've also received death threats - and so have some of my team-mates". She added: "We were giving a minute's silence to someone who committed domestic violence, for me, that's something that my feminist ideals can't allow: a tribute to Maradona. For me, he was an incredible player, but as a person, he left a lot to be desired."

THE VIEW FROM ENGLAND

The Hand of God goal! Well, what hasn't been said about it? How the 5ft 5in Diego Maradona leaped into the air and punched the ball over the much taller England keeper Peter Shilton and into the net. The referee didn't spot the handball despite furious England protests and four minutes later, Maradona glided all the way from his own half to score again Talking afterwards Maradona described the first goal as "a little with his head and a little with the hand of God." It was a title that stuck and the incident remains perhaps the most controversial incident in World Cup history.

Yet all these years later, there are some that cannot let that goal rest, nor let Diego rest in peace. While many who perhaps considered it a blot on Maradona's career yet thought that the moment of his death was possibly not the right time to re-open the debate, two members of the England team that day in Mexico grasped the nettle.

Lineker paid a lengthy tribute Diego during BT Sport's Champions League programme the night of the megastar's death. Lineker was preparing to host BT Sport's European coverage when news of Maradona's death broke. He had been part of the England team which was knocked out of the 1986 World Cup by those two Maradona goals – one of them the infamous 'Hand of God' effort, the other considered one of the greatest goals of all-time. Alongside pundits Michael Owen, Rio Ferdinand and Peter Crouch he recalled tales of Diego's genius. "I never thought in my lifetime that I would see anyone come remotely close to Diego in terms of their ability with a football. I think we've seen Messi, who is similar in many ways, both Argentinian, diminutive, brilliant left-foot. But Diego was incredible.

"I actually played with him as well for a half a game at Wembley against an English league side. I played for the 'Rest of the World' because I was at Barcelona at the time. All the players, people like Platini on the pitch, great players from all around the world, and everyone was totally in awe of him. I've just never seen anyone have such a beautiful affection with a football. People talk about the Hand of God goal, but the other goal he scored in that game. To do what he did, that little pivot on the halfway line and then to go past the players like they weren't there was just the most remarkable thing. It was the closest in my life I've ever felt like I ought to have applauded someone else scoring a goal. He was head and shoulders the best player of my generation."

However, his instant trigger happy tweet, didn't go down well. He was forced to defend himself on social media after his tribute to Diego received what he must have considered an unexpected backlash.

As news broke, Lineker was among the first to extend his sympathy and label Maradona "arguably the greatest of all-time". Lineker tweeted: "Reports from Argentina that Diego Armando Maradona has died. By some distance the best player of my generation and arguably the greatest of all time. After a blessed but troubled life, hopefully he'll finally find some comfort in the hands of God. #RIPDiego."

Despite his praise, some were left angry with his reference to the infamous 'Hand of God' goal. Brazilian journalist Eduardo Monsanto said: "Show some respect. Being an a★★hole does not fit you, or so I thought."

Lineker defended his tweet replying: "Sorry, where's the disrespect?'"

The Brazilian continued the conversation: "Come on... we both know what you meant. There's an entire country mourning the loss of their favourite son. This is no time for double meaning..."

"Your misunderstanding is complete," Lineker responded.

Another stated: "Not the time to make puns Gary". He replied: "Don't be ridiculous. It's heartfelt."

In response to a later tweet defending him, the former England striker said: "'Thank you. Can only imagine it's a translation issue." In the run-up to the 2006 World Cup, Lineker had tracked down Maradona for a documentary. When they first shook hands, Lineker said: "Which hand was it, this one?" As Maradona played along and lifted his left hand. Yet for all the controversy and the trauma of being on the losing side to a flagrant bit of cheating, the England striker still felt the Argentinian was "by some distance, the best player of my generation and arguably the greatest of all time".

On the other side of the argument stood Peter Shilton who found it hard to forgive Maradona not just for the incident itself but because he "never apologised" for his 'Hand of God' goal, but reiterating his well know and publicised views, fewer than 24 hours after his death was always going to be provocative.

Shilton made it clear it was something that continued to haunt him all these years later. "My life has long been linked with that of Diego Maradona — and not in the way I would have liked," Shilton wrote in and exclusive first person article in the *Daily Mail* having rejected a much bigger offer for a far more provocative interview with *The Sun* "but I am saddened to hear of his passing at such a young age. He was undoubtedly the greatest player I ever faced and my thoughts are with his family."

Of the incident Shilton recalled, "none of us expected what happened next. How could we? He challenged me for a high, looping ball, but knew he wouldn't get it with his head, so he punched it into the net. A clear offence. Cheating. As he ran away to celebrate he even looked back twice, as if waiting for the referee's whistle. He knew what he had done. Everybody did — apart from the referee and two linesmen."

This is the core of this book's argument. Was Diego a Hero or Villain? To many English eyes he remains a villain for sure, yet even some Englishmen can overlook the first goal with the staggering beauty and perfection of the 'Goal of the Century' just four minutes later. Lineker managed to pull a goal back in the final 10 minutes but their World Cup exit was confirmed, and captain on the day Shilton believes that without the first goal, Maradona would never have scored the second. "I don't care what anybody says, it won the game for Argentina," he added. "He scored a brilliant second almost immediately, but we were still reeling from what had happened minutes earlier. For the first time in the game, we let him get a run on us and he scored. It was a great goal but we were in no doubt — without the first goal he would not have scored the second."

Shilton never spoke to Maradona again after that despite several attempts, and lucrative offers, to have them appear together. England's most-capped player in history said that he would only appear with the Argentine if he gave an indication that he would apologise, but that contingency of an offer of an apology never arrived. "What I don't like is that he never apologised," said Shilton. "Never at any stage did he say he had cheated and that he would like to say sorry. Instead, he used his 'Hand of God' line. That wasn't right. It seems he had greatness in him but sadly no sportsmanship."

The next morning on *Good Morning Britain*, Gazza teased Shilton over the Hand of God goal by suggesting the incident had 'made' the England goalkeeper's career. Gazza, who played for England with Shilton in the years after that quarter-final, joked that it made the record caps holder famous when he said: "He was an icon, wasn't he? People go on about the Hand of God, but it made Peter Shilton anyway. Shilts, it made you, that goal." GMB hosts Ben Shephard and Susanna Reid burst into laughter, while Gascoigne giggled.

The 71-year-old Shilton looked somewhat less pleased and joked about his long time in the game after the episode. He replied: "Thanks for that Gazza, I did play for another 20 years or so after that."

Shilton again recalled that famous clash in Mexico. He noted: "We all knew he was a brilliant player. We didn't make any plans to stop him, whoever was close to him, was told to get close to him and stop him. We kept him very quiet until the goal, the Hand of God goal, the cheating goal. As I said we lost concentration for the second goal and he took advantage of that. A lot of the players at the time were very aggrieved at Maradona and one or two players to this day said they wouldn't shake hands with him, I never had the chance to meet him. It's so sad through addiction that his life's been taken so early. He had such a full life to live. It is sad."

NAPOLI - DIEGO'S MIRACLE

"You leave us with a great testament of what it means to be a man of fragility, strength and absolute love for life and one's neighbour. Your weaknesses, your imperfections, your mistakes are tantamount to your immense greatness."
Aurelio de Laurentiis, Napoli owner

"Diego Maradona is a God to the people of Naples. Maradona changed history. In 80 years, we had always suffered, fighting against relegation, yet in seven seasons with him we won two leagues, a UEFA Cup, two Italian Cups. I'm a fan too and to live those years with Maradona was incredible. — those are the words of Naples native Fabio Cannavaro, who was in the youth ranks at Napoli when Maradona was there and later won the World Cup with Italy in 2006, when he described how one man changed the face of history for that southern Italian club as Maradona salvaged his club career after a disappointing spell with Barcelona.

Flags were flown at half-mast outside the ground of another of his former clubs, Barcelona, while Boca Juniors switched off all the lights at their 'La Bombonera' stadium, except those in Maradona's private box. It was from there that Diego Maradona left Argentina in a world record £5million transfer for Barcelona but the big money move, and the high expectations, never worked out. In fact, it ended in an incident even worse that that infamous Eric Cantona episode at Crystal Palace.

Barcelona lost the La Liga title to Athletic Bilbao by a solitary point in 1983-84, a point they would have certainly made up and easily surpassed had Maradona not had his ankle broken by Bilbao's hardman Andoni Goikoetxea, aptly named 'The Butcher of Bilbao" during an early-season meeting.

When the two sides then met in the Copa del Rey final after the conclusion of the title race, Bilbao again came out on top. When Bilbao's Miguel Sola told Diego to 'f*** off' on the final whistle, Maradona went crazy, eager for revenge. He squared up to Sola and headbutted him before all hell broke loose. Maradona elbowed another Bilbao player in the face and kneed another in the head, knocking him out. With a series of karate kicks aimed at any opponent within range, his Barca team-mates joined in.

King Juan Carlos was among 100,000 fans inside the Bernabeu watching as a riot broke out with 60 people injured when fans started throwing objects from the stands. It was Maradona's final game for Barcelona, who decided they couldn't tolerate any more and sold him to Napoli for a world record £6.9m.

Maradona's arrival at Napoli's Sao Paolo stadium was seen by 75,000 fans and Diego was instantly regarded as the saviour of the struggling Serie A club. There was a pronounced north south divide in the country with the southerners definitely the poorer neighbours so when Diego finally delivered the Serie A title in 1987 it led to summer long celebrations in the city and mock funerals for northern rivals Inter, AC and most of all Juventus.

Maradona's face adorned murals in the city and sudden rise in the birth rate following the triumph saw thousands of children named after him. Diego would go on to win another title in 1990 and a UEFA Cup in 1991 but within weeks of that triumph he was banned from the sport for 15 months following a drug violation. By this point Maradona was a regular cocaine user, and was treated for addiction.

It was little wonder in the hours following his death thousands of Napoli fans gathered at the Sao Paolo to pay their respects to a man regarded as a God in the city. The magical trophy laden seven years Maradona spent at Napoli were by far the most successful of his club career. This unfashionable Italian club had an affinity with Diego's impoverished background, and they had never witnessed anything like such success or possessed the most recognisable and best player in world football.

Carlo Ancelotti said Maradona's legacy will be shaped by winning the World Cup almost single-handedly, not by the "Hand of God", as he paid tribute to the "best player I ever played against".

The Everton manager faced him several times when Milan and Napoli were title rivals and admitted meting out "strong contact" but Maradona never complained. They later became good friends, and Ancelotti experienced at first hand the devotion Maradona inspired in Naples when he became Napoli coach. "He was my opponent and then he became my friend," Ancelotti said. "He was very humble and it is a big loss for football, but the memories will always be there. He was a fantastic player who helped football around the world. At this time he was the best player in the world, and the best player I ever played against. He was so difficult to stop and had unbelievable quality. He never complained on the pitch. I tried to stop him with strong contact but he never complained and after that we became good friends. We met at events after our playing careers were finished and it was always good to spend time with him. He was not only a footballer but a great example to show everywhere. But this is the life. I will always keep fantastic memories of him."

Ancelotti was asked by a Colombian journalist whether, in light of some English newspapers reporting Maradona's death with "Hand of God" photos on their front pages, he accepted their assessment of the icon as a cheat. "It was a handball in a big game but the referee missed it. You cannot explain Maradona with a handball! You have to explain Maradona by what he did and I think that World Cup, and I was there in '86 but I never played, he practically won it alone. Of course Argentina had fantastic players in their team like Burruchaga and Valdano but Maradona practically won that World Cup alone."

There was never a dull moment of the pitch, full of wonderful goals and match winning performances, and off it there was little difference, it was wild and exciting times for Diego. With the status of a demi-God by the people of the city, he couldn't go anywhere without being surrounded, hero-worshipped. Hooked on cocaine since his Barcelona days, Diego soon sought the services of the Camorra – the city's notorious mafia - who offered him protection in the city. They also increasingly indulged his habits of partying, drug-taking and extra-marital affairs but even all this had to be fitted into some sort of schedule to get him into a fit state to actually play football once a week!

Maradona's week for most of the time he spent with them was pretty routine; Serie A match on a Sunday, Sunday night until Wednesday morning continuous partying and cocaine binges, Wednesday morning until Saturday evening was 'cleanse', sweating it all out of his system in training ready for the next match on a Sunday. The routine was revealed in Asif Kapadia's 2019 documentary about Maradona's time with Napoli. Inevitably, it proved his downfall. After a phone call with a prostitute was tapped by the police in January 1991, charges were brought against Maradona for cocaine possession and distribution. A blood test in April of that year found traces of the drug and a 15-month ban from football, leading Maradona to flee to Argentina.

Maradona's first 'Hand of God' goal was scored in Italy, and Brazil legend Zico was suspended for four games for protesting the referee's decision to give the goal. The former Brazil international recalls how Maradona escaped punishment for handling the ball into the net two years *before* the infamous punch over Peter Shilton when playing for Napoli against Udinese. Zico was red carded for sarcastically applauding the referee after the goal was given. "It was 1984, I had just arrived in Udine. I didn't play in Naples and he scored a brace," he told Italian sports paper *Gazzetta Dello Sport.* "We were 2-1 up but Diego scored the equaliser. The game was almost finished when they hit the crossbar and Diego anticipated our goalkeeper scoring with his hand. The ref and his assistant didn't notice it. I was furious, I ran behind the referee and I told him: 'Congratulations, continue like this, you are doing well.' I was sent off and suspended for four games. I often joked with him about his goal, I used to tell him: 'You trained the

Hand of God with us.' He said: 'You are the good part of football, I am the bad one.'" Asked where he ranked Maradona, Zico commented: "Maradona is among the best five players I've ever seen: Garrincha, Pele, Diego, Cruyff and Beckenbauer."

Yet thirty years on from his reign in the city, such was Diego's status that people defied a coronavirus lockdown to pay tribute, ahead of Napoli's closed-door Europa League fixture against the Croatian team Rijeka. The home team, who all stepped onto the pitch wearing black armbands and Maradona's No. 10 jersey, won the match 2-0. The grieving became a global phenomenon, but the news created as many tears in that part of Italy as it did throughout Argentina. To show their respect for what he had achieved, the Stadio San Paolo was illuminated in Maradona's honour that night. A minute's silence was held before the match against Rijeka. "He was unique, he represented everything, everything for us Neapolitans," fan Gianni Autiero told Reuters. "I have cried for only a few people in my life, and Diego is one of them."

Before Napoli kicked off against Roma only four days after Diego's death, captain Lorenzo Insigne went on a lap of the Stadio San Paolo, placing bouquets of flowers beneath the empty stands behind each goal. From the Curva A hung a banner prepared by fans: "Your death comes as a blow to the chest," it read. "A pain in the heart. Naples swears you eternal love.

A minutes silence was observed before kick-off, and the game was paused in the 10th minute so that both teams could offer up a further 60 seconds of applause. Napoli were playing in a special blue-and-white striped kit, designed to pay homage to Maradona's Argentina. Earlier in the day, the mayor of Naples confirmed that this stadium will be renamed after the player. For four days, fans had come to light a candle and say a prayer before the mural of Maradona in via Emanuele de Deo. Corrado Ferlaino, the man who signed him as Napoli president, made his own pilgrimage there, followed by the legendary Roma winger Bruno Conti. After a free-kick scored by Lorenzo Insigne after half an hour, the club's website paid another tribute, "not just a goal, but a citation." Napoli's captain, the only Neapolitan in their team, commented: "Our idol is gone, and it hurts. Today we wanted to put on a great show and get the right result for him and this city, which is suffering."

During his post-game interview on Sky Sport, the manager redirected another question about Maradona into an answer about the ongoing pandemic. "The air we breathe is sad," he said, "but in my opinion right now the city needs to have good sense too. There are too many people without masks. Maradona is a legend. Everyone in Naples knows who he is. But, in this moment, we need to be smart, or we will all pay the consequences. I understand the affection, I understand the atmosphere. But I hope that from tomorrow people will start to do what they should, because it's a shame, the city is suffering a lot." *Corriere dello Sport* ran the front-page headline declaring that "Maradona won". But these were goals, as the website Napolista put it, "in his style".

Lawyer Angelo Pisani saved Maradona from the Italian tax authorities by giving the 'Pibe de Oro' the opportunity to return freely to Italy without the risk of having his earrings or Rolex torn off his wrist for tax evasion. Speaking in an exclusive interview with *MailOnline* Pisani was disturbed how Maradona died alone when he said, 'From what we learn from the media in Argentina he died alone, incredible, that he slept alone without the presence and affection of family members after a surgical intervention. This is crazy. In Napoli he would not have died alone at home. Delays in medical aid will be ascertained but it is not normal that no one slept with him that evening. Everyone tells me that Maradona was alone on the last night. I think it's absurd. He had undergone a delicate brain surgery a few days ago. He had just been operated on his brain: he needed to have love. His son Diego Junior would have been there near him had he not had Covid, he would have been next to him and would have showered him with affection and love. I don't think it was like that in Argentina. Diego Junior must know how his father died. We need to clarify. The boy loved his father and now is suffering. Diego fell asleep alone and it is still not clear how he died. In Napoli he had real friends: he would have had the vigil and prayer of supporters outside his home, he would have had everyone close to him if he had chosen to be treated in Italy and in Napoli."

A city of 2.8 million inhabitants had unflinching, total affection and love for Diego, "Napoli was the only city where Diego was happy. When I think about our video call while running on the treadmill, I feel like crying. We had to lose weight together: it was his bet. He gave me such a big smile that I will never forget it. He shouted at me: "Angelone if you eat I see you!". It was he who asked how my son was born a few months. It was full of love.'

Napoli owner Aurelio de Laurentiis wrote in an open letter that he wants to rename the stadium after Maradona. The mayor of Naples, Luigi de Magistris, backed the idea. In a letter paying tribute to Maradona, De Laurentiis wrote: "You leave us with a great testament of what it means to be a man of fragility, strength and absolute love for life and one's neighbour. Your weaknesses, your imperfections, your mistakes are tantamount to your immense greatness. I believe it is right to name the San Paolo after you, so we can keep you with us as a witness of the excellent path this team has taken," De Laurentiis added. "Thank you, Diego. You are, and will always be, with all of us."

Italian law typically requires a person to have been dead for 10 years before a communally owned facility can be named after them, but the expectation is that the rule will be waived. A subway stop near to the ground is also expected to take Maradona's name. As the Mayor of Naples, Luigi de Magistris explained it: "In this way, we can have another station dedicated to art."

Dries Mertens said it was "tough to pull that shirt on" after the Napoli side all wore Diego Maradona's legendary No. 10 shirt before the Europa League match against Rijeka. As fans gathering outside the Stadio San Paolo to lay flowers, sing his name and let off flares and fireworks before the players paid their own respects in a minute's silence. Captain Lorenzo Insigne also laid a wreath before kick-off, while the Napoli team lined up in the iconic and long-retired 'Maradona 10' shirts before their 2-0 win over the Croatian side. Mertens said that although the tributes were emotional for the players he is glad they honoured Maradona's impact on the city of Naples. "It was an awful moment for me, so I can only imagine how those who lived through his time at Napoli must have felt. He made such a big impact on this city and for everyone in the south of Italy. I want to be positive, and focus on my memories of a smiling man who loved football. It was tough to pull that shirt on. In some ways, it was always a dream, but not like this."

Mertens, who joined the club in 2013 from PSV Eindhoven, is Napoli's all-time leading goalscorer with 128, having overtaken Maradona's tally of 115 last year. The Belgian star apologised to the Argentinian great for his own achievements ever being compared to his. "You were the first thing that came to my mind when I signed for Naples. Wearing the blue shirt will mean even more from now on," he commented on Instagram. "Napoli lost part of its soul today. You were, and will always be, an inspiration to all of us. If my name has ever been placed next to yours, I apologise, I will never be at your level. What you did for 'our' city will go down in history forever. It was an honour to have met you. Forever my idol." Asked about his apology, Mertens said: "I apologised to him, because my name was used in the same sentence as his and that's not right. He was and always will be unique."

Marseille manager Andre Villas-Boas, once manager at Chelsea and Tottenham, called on FIFA to retire the number 10 shirt from the game. Maradona's former club Napoli had not used the No 10 shirt since 2000 as a mark of respect for the player who guided them to several trophies and Villas-Boas said global soccer body FIFA should also pay tribute by withdrawing the number. "Maradona, yes it is tough news, I would like FIFA to retire the number 10 shirt in all competitions, for all teams," Villas-Boas told reporters after Marseille's 2-0 Champions League defeat by Porto. "It would be the best homage we could do for him. He is an incredible loss for the world of football." FIFA has previously said it would not allow Argentina to dispense with the number.

Paul Gascoigne recalled a remarkable encounter with Maradona while playing for Lazio. Before a pre-season friendly between his side and the Argentine's Sevilla in 1992 he exchanged pleasantries with the Argentinian genius in the tunnel. "I remember Lazio wanted us to play against Sevilla and Maradona, and I said, 'No I want to play against Juventus'. But the president wanted to play against Maradona. So I went, 'Okay then, I'll meet you there'.

THE INCREDIBLE STORY OF SEVILLE

Maradona's impact at Napoli had been so great that during the 1990 World Cup Neopolitans ended up cheering against their own country! Hosts Italy had been drawn to play most of their games in Rome but the semi-final was in the Sao Paolo and the opponents were Argentina captained by the God of Naples himself. After a tense encounter ended 1-1 the game went to penalties with Maradona scoring before Aldo Serena's miss for the hosts. But the support the home crowd gave for Italy's opponents that night has often caused friction with the rest of the country.

Within 18 months Maradona's stay at Napoli came to an abrupt end following positive tests for cocaine that led to a 15-month suspension from FIFA. Adam Bate painted a vivid picture of his remarkable season at Seville in an article for *Sky Sports*. He discussed how Sevilla president Luis Cuervas promised to deliver Maradona but an offer of £2.5m was rejected. Managed by Diego's World Cup winning manager Carlos Bilardo, Sevilla hoped to get the best out of Maradona by building a team around him, Bilardo even threatened to walk out if his star man did not arrive but the season began without him. It took the intervention of Sepp Blatter and FIFA to strike a deal. They wanted Maradona to return in good time for the 1994 World Cup. During a remarkable five-hour meeting at FIFA headquarters, with Blatter mediating, the world governing body helped strike a deal. Much of the £4.5m fee would be covered by Silvio Berlusconi's Italian media company on the guarantee that Maradona's Sevilla commit to playing a series of showpiece friendlies around the world.

In late September 1992, Diego arrived and Bilardo explained to the squad in a famous team meeting, that they were in the background; this was the Maradona show, put their faith in his genius, it could be special. "That first session he went out full of enthusiasm with his boots untied, laces dangling, which isn't a great idea: you fall, you can't hit the ball properly, it's dangerous," then-club-captain Manolo Jimenez tells ESPN. "But not to him. He didn't fall. Instead, there was mastery. He was different."

Jimenez handed over the captaincy after defender Juan Martagon argued that nobody could imagine Maradona without the armband. Training was moved from the morning to the afternoon on Bilardo's instruction. It was suspected that Maradona's nocturnal habits were to blame. Maradona arrived with his usual large entourage and, while still living in a city hotel, crashed his Mercedes at 2am. Yet Sevilla enjoyed a fine start to the season but some couldn't stomach some of the extraordinary antics of the now overweight, egotistical, and ageing star despite the desire to get the best out of him. Soon after the car crash, Diego moved into the villa of Juan Antonio Ruiz Roman, famous bullfighter in the world, who went by the nickname of Spartacus.

The adventure began against Bayern Munich on September 28, 1992. The hastily arranged friendly saw chaos at the Ramon Sanchez Pizjuan stadium as Diego Maradona played his first game for the club which Sevilla won 3-1. His barber replicated his haircut from Mexico '86, and at first, there was a chance he might play like he did back then but it didn't last long. Paul Gascoigne's Lazio were the opponents in November for another friendly when Paul Gascoigne scored in a 1-1 draw. Maradona went close with a bicycle kick and almost netted the winner when a free-kick struck the crossbar with two minutes left.

A 2-0 victory over Real Madrid in December was inspired by Maradona. Davor Suker scored Sevilla's opening goal and would go on to win the Champions League with Real Madrid before becoming top scorer at the 1998 World Cup. "When I was a kid I used to watch Diego on television in my room," the Croatian striker would later recall. "Suddenly I found myself sharing breakfast, training and a locker room with him. I was hoping he would teach me something and then, finally, he called me. He said: 'I don't want you to run to the sides or anything. Just keep your head down, run towards the goalkeeper, and I will give it you there'. Very few players in the world can say that but he was one. If you watch my goals for Sevilla, they always came the same way. It is something that will stay with me forever."

There were more friendlies against Sao Paulo and Porto, Galatasaray in Istanbul, before Maradona returned to Buenos Aires for a game against his old club Boca. "I had not seen fanaticism until I saw that," said Prieto. In La Liga, Maradona scored the winning penalty on his home league debut against Real Zaragoza, when he spotted a tin foil rolled sandwich wrapper, shaped like a ball, when taking a corner. He flicked it up and juggled it. "He did it several times in training," said team-mate Rafa Paz. "He'd see a lemon on the ground and he would pick it up with his foot and hold it until he was bored. Imagine the rest of the team. There were those who tried when Diego was not there. It was impossible."

His team-mates adored him. Monchi, later to become the club's sporting director, remembers Maradona taking one look at his fake Rolex and buying him a real one, others were given shirts or the opportunity to take one of his many fast cars for a spin. There were late night dinners and parties. "It was joy and happiness," said Diego Simeone, the Atletico Madrid coach and fellow Argentine, who was then a young midfielder at Sevilla. "Maradona's arrival at Seville at that time was a very important step, an important moment for the team. Many of the young boys felt sheltered by him. It made us grow and I am grateful for the times that I have lived football with Maradona."

"To live alongside him was a privilege," Monchi told ESPN. "He was a childhood hero of mine, so you can't imagine what it was like when he became a teammate. I remember the first day he came. We're all in the dining room of the team hotel and in walks Diego, and we all thought the same thing: 'He's come to play with me!' 'He's going to be on my team!' Then you get know him day-to-day and he was just incredible.

"People think of him as this great individual but that forgets that he was also very much a team man. He stood alongside his team-mates and believed in the importance of that solidarity. He was the first one to stand up and fight for win bonuses for the team even though it was probably nothing to him and survival for me. If there was a problem with our travel, he was the first one to make sure it was put right. He was a 10 out of 10 as person. And we know that as a footballer he was a 20.'

Ciro Ferrara was team-mates with Maradona for seven years at Napoli. The former defender told Republica: 'I respected him, I knew him as few in the world but I loved him like many fans: it was impossible not to. Maradona was a person good and deep, he had an overflowing humanity. Diego was close to everyone. He was a God, no one has ever been more human than him. Sometimes at night I could hear the roar of his Ferrari coming from his garage. Then the next day when he was late for training, my team-mates asked "so Ciro, what's he doing?" and I'd say "I don't think he's coming today". But then I found him training alone, like a madman. He worked really hard, he was all for one and one for all. He made me win and he made me become a man.'

Such was his form at Sevilla that Argentina manager Alfio Basile, recalled Maradona after two years out of the team, but he was needed by his club for a match against Logrones, so instead Maradona departed without the club's permission. After the fall out, his visits to training became less frequent. There were reports that Maradona was being tracked by a private detective – a dossier was being constructed that would see him denied any pay off as Seville wanted rid of him. Maradona drove his Porsche at high speed through the city and was caught by police. "A dreadful year could not have ended worse, with the loss of an icon and a friend," Jimenez says. "I will always say, 'I played with Maradona,' and for me that's like winning a trophy. To be able to play with him, talk to him, listen to him, have him listen to you - not everyone can say that. That's a medal. He taught us a lot, in good times and bad."

In Maradona's final home game, a 1-1 draw against Burgos, early in the second half, Bilardo substituted him, the manager receiving a volley of abuse. He never played for Sevilla again and left on June 23, 1993 with the team finishing seventh.

Bilardo and Maradona eventually came to blows. As Maradona put it, "We kicked the sh*t out of each other." Maradona was still only 31. There was time for another glorious chapter and he was being reunited with the man who had guided Argentina to that World Cup win in 1986. But the fight ended Maradona's time in Spain. He left Sevilla after a single season, notable only for his drug use, trips to brothels, a tale of bullfighters, ball juggling, private detectives and public partying.

He managed only five goals in 26 games, filed a law suit because of the unpaid money that he felt he was owed in his contract before he returned to Argentina, after a season that was best forgotten. He made it to his fourth World Cup, scoring with a memorable strike against Greece, but was soon sent home in disgrace for a doping offence.

THE DAY I MET DIEGO

"Typical Diego, always asleep, always late" Ossie Ardiles.

Ossie was panicking. Diego was still fast asleep in his hotel bedroom and Ossie was pacing up and down the hotel lobby. I was watching the drama unfold and thought it was like something from a John Cleese script as I started pacing up and down alongside Ossie. But that didn't seem to calm him down, it just made him even more anxious.

"Typical Diego", moaned Ossie, one of the great man's true friends and confidantes, and clearly someone willing to put up with Diego's foibles, "always asleep, always late".

This was an important assignment not just for Ossie but also for me. For Ossie, it was his own glorious testimonial at White Hart Lane and he had arranged for none other than Diego Maradona to play at the Lane. For my part, I had managed to twist Ossie's arm into getting an exclusive interview with Diego Maradona, and you don't get that too often in a journalistic career, in fact it was a once in a life time opportunity.

The whole scenario seemed so unlikely. Diego was the star of the Argentina national team about to embark on the 1986 World Cup Finals, only a matter of 10 weeks away, and Argentina were in between two friendlies in Denmark and Israel, so Diego was supposed to be jetting off with the squad from Copenhagen to Tel Aviv. But Diego had promised his great friend Ossie he would turn out for Spurs in his testimonial and despite protests from Argentine manager Carlos Bilardo who told him in no uncertain terms he wasn't given permission to leave the camp, Diego, being a law unto himself, waved them all goodbye and hopped on a flight to London, along with his wife, minders, agents and a multitude of mates and hangers-on - enough of them to boost the gate all on their own.

Ossie told me that if I wanted to interview Diego, and at best, it would only be for a few minutes, with Ossie interpreting, it would be on condition that I turn up early at the central London hotel where he was staying, as the plan was to leave early to beat the usual bottleneck traffic along the Seven Sisters Road so synonymous with match days at the Lane. Ossie didn't want a journalist, a photographer, and an eager newspaper delaying Diego and his appearance at the Lane. After a quick chat in the afternoon, Ossie envisaged a chat with his old mate over afternoon tea before heading off to the stadium.

Yet no matter how many times Ossie tried to get the concierge to ring the room, he failed to get through. Diego had taken all phones off the hook so he could get some sleep after his match the previous night and his journey form Copenhagen to London the next morning.

Two o'clock, became three o'clock then four and five and with each passing hour Ossie became more fraught. When it reached five, Ossie made it clear there would be no bloody (or words to that effect) interview, there just wouldn't be time!

Eventually Diego emerged from the hotel lift into the reception unannounced, so it was quite an entry, as he wasn't alone in that lift, as out spilled his wife, his minders, his agents and all his mates. It reminded me of the old advert for the Mini, to see how many people could squeeze into that tiny car! This must have warranted an entry into the Guinness Book of Records for the number of people who could squeeze into a hotel lift.

There was hardly enough time to make it to ground, at best to make it for kick off, but no time for any warm up or anything else. As for my interview. "No chance!" snapped a very worried Ossie.

Now, I don't usually beg, but I thought this was the only chance, to pull on the heart strings of a very genuine friend in Ossie. I told him the *Daily Mirror* was keeping five pages open at the back of the paper for the interview, two double page spreads and the back page and if I let them down at such a late stage, I might be looking for another job.

Ossie suggested that I accompanied them to the ground. "What about the picture?" I asked. Again I cannot repeat what

Ossie said, but he had definitely picked up the language of the dressing room but by now the poor man who was only here to take a couple of pictures that shouldn't have taken more than a minute had been here for three hours! Ossie made it plain there wouldn't be a couple of pictures, just time for one. He relented. We went outside the hotel as the photographer insisted on better light - again, that didn't go down too well. But out we all trotted, Diego, his bemused missus, Ossie and myself, for a picture that not only made the Mirror's pages, but has pride of place on my wall alongside pictures of myself with the likes of Pelé, Sir Bobby Charlton, Ruud Gullit, Glenn Hoddle, Sir Stanley Matthews, and Claudio Ranieri, among others.

Quick as a flash the one picture was taken, all requests for the usual photographers cry of 'just one more", was ignored, and it happened so fast, I can hardly recall much more, as the next thing I can remember is that Ossie was driving, Diego was in the front passenger seat, and I was behind them armed with my note book and pen - no mobiles in those days so I couldn't even let the office know what was happening. Diego's not insubstantial entourage crammed into a couple of giant limos and followed us.

I asked the questions and Ossie translated as he drove, but it occurred to me that the two of them discussed my questions before Diego gave his answers to Ossie, but I am sure Ossie told him that he had known me for some time and trusted me and that his words wouldn't be distorted in the English media, especially so close to the World Cup. I trusted Ossie to give me as near as damn it the answers Diego provided, but equally I am sure Ossie helped him and advised him on what would be appropriate to say.

Diego was just a kid when he first got into the national side and Ossie looked after him, like a father figure, and Diego trusted Ossie's judgement but even in the bizarre world of Diego Maradona, I can only imagine this was the first, and only time, he shared a car with a journalist, and felt comfortable in their presence, as later on he would be shooting them!

I asked Diego if, one day, he would be open to playing in

English football, and whether playing in Ossie's testimonial might not be the last time we see him playing in our country. He seemed very open to the idea, especially with Ossie in English football, and if he played for any English club it would have to be Spurs. As you can imagine, for a tabloid like the *Mirror* this was heaven sent and would make the back page and one of the spreads already.

As for the game, I clearly missed the kick off and in fact I only managed to make it to the press box for the start of the second half.

As for Diego he came unprepared and had to borrow a pair of Clive Allen's boots as Allen recalls "Ossie says: 'Who takes six and a half?'" "I tell him I do and that I had two pairs of boots; one old pair I'd worn all season and a new pair I was breaking in, so I said: 'Diego, be my guest and take whatever pair you want!'"

Glenn Hoddle, who played alongside Maradona in midfield as Spurs won 2-1 against Inter Milan, recalls, "the sheer magnetism of Maradona lifted the whole atmosphere. A staggering 30,000-plus crowd turned up for the match, and the kick-off had to be delayed for 15 minutes to allow all the thousands of fans in. Maradona and Ossie entered the stadium after the two teams to thunderous applause. It was clear the public were enthralled to have the chance to see a player of Maradona's skill and he didn't disappoint them. Of course he did not extend himself to the full, but I am a player whose philosophy is built around skilful football and I could nothing but admire this stocky little genius."

As well as being Maradona's opponent during his playing days, Hoddle loved being alongside Maradona played during Tottenham legend Ossie Ardiles' testimonial in 1986 just priot to the World Cup Finals. They enjoyed a special connection on the pitch that day and it was one of the more memorable evenings in his career. Hoddle added: 'That night at White Hart Lane for Ossie's testimonial, it was fabulous to play with him. As soon as we got on the pitch, we just gelled. It was an incredible evening and I loved every minute of it. It was a sad loss for football. The wonderful genius of the player, what he did with the football, it was like the ball was born with him - there was one attached to his foot.

"It was a wonderful night. Testimonials can sometimes be a very low-key occasions. This was a full house, Inter Milan came over, it was a really good game and with Maradona playing the atmosphere was incredible. When Ossie brought him in the dressing room he did not know any English and I did not know too much Spanish, so we ended up nodding and stuff like that. I gave him the No 10 shirt to wear and I wore the No 11 shirt on the night. It was wonderful. As soon as we went out on the pitch and the ball came out, it was almost like the football was our interpreter and we had a little bit of a connection. It was fascinating playing with him and a great honour. We just gelled. It is amazing what football does, it breaks down language barriers. It was a magical night.

Hoddle described Maradona as 'the greatest player who touched the planet'. Hoddle was on the pitch that day and recalled his emotions after seeing Maradona go from a 'rascal' to a 'genius'. The former England manager said: 'I remember hitting the ball with his arm, with his hand, and then flicking his head. It was very sneaky with what he did there. The referee didn't spot it, I was trying to catch the referee, not all the players have sold it. It was the rascal in him that did that. Then the second goal was out of this world. In many ways that summed up Diego. The first the with the rascal and then the genius with that goal. The pitch was awful, the long grass, the rutty turf at the bottom. To score that goal and keep it under that control was genius. He was the greatest player that touched this planet."

Hoddle believes that if VAR was in use at the time, the wonder goal might have been ruled out because of a foul on him in the build up, although he concedes it was a border line decision. He explains: "I'll tell you what, there is a little debate because if you watch on the tape, I think I was fouled. It was a sort of a

50-50 decision, and from that the ball spins out to Diego, but I've stopped and sort of appealed. I got myself up off the floor because I had been brought down, but I'm now the wrong side of our goal and retreating but he's off going past everybody the way he did and then poked it past Peter, it's quite incredible, it really was. You don't catch in on telly because it was that quick, and form there he goes on that amazing run. I saw it long afterwards, but on the say we spoke about it only very quickly."

As for where Glenn would put Argentinian in the pantheon of players, he is in doubt… "For me, he was the best player on the planet at the time and the best I have ever seen - even better than Cristiano Ronaldo and Lionel Messi. What he could do on these pitches now would be phenomenal, and with the rules as well. So yeah, it has got to be Maradona. It is always difficult to compare different eras of football. I did not see the best of Pelé so it is very difficult to judge. There was Johan Cruyff, some wonderful players. But sometimes you have to judge what it would be like the other way around. Maybe not Maradona playing in this era, I think about Messi and Ronaldo going back to the 1980s and doing what Maradona did with a football. He used to get kicked to bits on bad pitches. The way he caressed the ball, it was like when he was born there was a football attached to his foot. It seemed as if it was so natural to him. He was only small and to show the strength and character he did . . . I put him above anyone else because of the rules at the time. He won the World Cup with a very average Argentina side and then went to Napoli and did what he did there."

Hoddle sent his condolences to Maradona's fans and family. Hoddle himself suffered a cardiac arrest in 2018 while preparing for BT Sport duty but pulled through and is still a pundit today. Hoddle said: "He died of a cardiac arrest, which is what I went through two years ago. He didn't have Simon Daniels there to help him because the cardiac arrest, you have a short period of time to get the aid that you need. I'm a very, very lucky man and hope Diego's family and everyone mourning him in Argentina at the moment, my thoughts are with everyone as I was close to going myself.'

Chris Waddle, also played in that game back in 1986 and remembers, "I've never seen a better footballer. Never. He was by far the best player I've ever played with. In the game he did a couple of nice runs and a bicycle kick; he was quite quiet, but when you had the ball you knew you could give it to him and there wouldn't be any problems. His touch was amazing and he was so strong. His change of pace and change of direction were incredible. His touch was amazing and he was so strong. His change of pace and change of direction were incredible."

In more recent times, Gary Lineker was fronting a documentary on Diego, and I was invited to be interviewed in a hotel in Covent Garden where they were filming, and that alone was going to make a nice headline for me, as it was certain that Diego would be asked by Gary about the Hand of God goal. There was much media speculation that Diego was being paid £50,000 for the interview, which was big bucks back then. The BBC executives at the time that I spoke to said it was much, much less, but no doubt it came close with all the travelling and expenditure involved, so at the time, it was a big budget documentary.

HOW DIEGO ALMOST SIGNED FOR SPURS...
AND SHEFFIELD UNITED

Teddy Sheringham recalls a conversation with his then manager Ossie Ardiles about how close Diego Maradona came to signing for the north London club. By this time Maradona was in the twilight years of his career following a spell at Sevilla. "I got on really well with Ossie, and I think I was the captain at the time, and he came to me one day and said 'I want your opinion, I'm thinking about signing someone'. And I was like 'go on' and he was like 'Diego Maradona', and I went 'Ossie, Ossie, really! Are you? Do it, just do it'. He said 'I'm in talks with him at the moment' and I was like 'my God, do it, it would be brilliant to play with him'. He came to me about three days later and was like 'I've decided not to sign Diego, he's got too much baggage around him'."

The disappointment of missing out on Maradona did not last long for Sheringham as World Cup winner Jürgen Klinsmann soon arrived. Sheringham added: "I couldn't believe that Jürgen had just won the World Cup and he was coming to Tottenham - and he was a revelation at Tottenham." Klinsmann scored 30 goals in his only season in the Premier League, helping fire Spurs to seventh in the table, before he went on to join Bayern Munich the following summer, but he would re-join in the 1997-98 season.

Gary Mabbutt recalls; "He was one of the greatest players in the world. Also during Ossie's time he tried to sign Mario Kempes for Spurs as well, I think. Obviously he had his Argentinian links and he was very good friends with these players. Kempes came on a pre-season tour with us but Diego never actually got to be a part of the club apart from playing in Ardiles' testimonial game."

Maradona played for Newell's Boys instead during the 93/94 season, before finishing his playing career with Boca Juniors in his home country.

It wasn't the first time that Diego had been linked to a move to England. Back in 1978 the then Sheffield United manager

Harry Haslam went to Argentina on a scouting mission in 1978 where he spotted17-year-old Maradona, then on the books at Argentinos Juniors where he had made his professional debut two years earlier. So impressed was Haslam that he offered £200,000 on the spot to bring this precocious talent to Yorkshire but the Blades' board, then in the Second Division, decided against backing Haslam's offer. The transfer fell through when the Second Division club failed to stump up extra cash on top of the fee, which would have doubled their investment, and that was far too much for them. Instead Haslam signed Maradona's compatriot Alex Sabella, a gifted midfielder from River Plate.

Harry Haslam's original plans was to sign Ricky Villa and Ossie Ardiles who had been earmarked for a £750,000 switch to South Yorkshire, only for Tottenham to profit when that deal also fell through and Haslam tipped off Keith Burkinshaw and Terry Neill. While Neill wanted Ardiles, he didn't want Villa, and Ossie didn't want to come to England without his compatriot. Neill was also chasing even bigger fish, he wanted Johan Cruyff and also Maradona but all of his work came to nothing as the Arsenal board, as Neill once told me, vetoed any foreign signings.

Even the signing of Ossie and Ricky is surrounded in mystery. I was told that after Haslam tipped off Burkinshaw about their availability, the Spurs manager, with his team freshly promoted to the First Division, wasn't keen on the pair, and he then asked Terry Neill to accompany him on the trip to buy Ricky Villa. At the last minute Terry Neill pulled out and left Burkinshaw to go it alone and fly out from Stansted airport with Haslam. Haslam and director John Hassle joined Burkinshaw and his party on a flight to Buenos Aires along with local journalist Tony Pritchett.

John Garrett, of Sheffield United's Legends Of The Lane, takes up the story. "Already out there for United was Oscar Arce, an Argentine who was a coach at United and had played for Villa in 1968. He was acting as an interpreter and Rattin, a legend at Boca Juniors, was also involved. The United travelling party were taken to the outskirts of Buenos Aires to a training ground to watch this kid put through his paces. Haslam was mesmerised by him and straight away said 'I'll take him, how much?' His club at the time wanted £150,000 for him, which was not the end of the world when you think we were just a year away from Nottingham Forest spending £1m on Trevor Francis. It was more than affordable for United and they were happy and wanted to do the deal. At the time, Argentina was run by the military junta, a right-wing coup that overthrew the then president. That night, Haslam's in his room relaxing thinking he's got this wonder kid and then gets a knock at the door from a member of the military police, someone like Eric Estrada in *Chips*, who has turned up at the hotel. He's saying that he has heard we're paying Boca £150,000 for this player and if United want the military to let Diego out of the country, they would like a payment of £150,000 too. So not only have you got a figure of £300,000, which I would imagine is getting towards a fair amount of cash for an untried 17-year-old, but the main problem was that it was starting to get a bit political. The total of £300,000 was not really a problem, United could afford it. But a bribe to the military police to get him out the country was not something United were comfortable with. Once the board of directors got wind of the fact that this was now getting a little bit hairy, they wanted nothing to do with it. It was never the money that was a problem. United weren't baulking on the money, had the club said £300k they would have paid it, it was just the minute the junta got involved United ran a mile. Historically over the years the managers have, generally speaking, been given the money to buy the players they wanted. United have always been famed for paying the right money and Ian Porterfield was one of the highest paid managers in the country at the time he was boss, so United have never really been afraid to spend money. It was just purely and simply the fact that the military junta had got involved and it scared United a little bit as to what they were getting involved in."

Haslam's son, Keith, remembers the extraordinary deal that "would have made Sheffield United". He told Sky Sports' Tim

Thornton, "My father was out in Argentina in Buenos Aires with a couple of his coaches, Danny Begara and Oscar Acre. He was trying to line up a deal with Ricky Villa and Ossie Ardiles but Sheffield United couldn't afford the money that was required at the time and Tottenham got them. My dad was looking around for another player and the super-kid at the time was Diego. They negotiated a deal, which was accepted, of £400,000, but the chairman of Sheffield United, John Hassell, said, 'There isn't a player at 18 worth £400,000, so we can't do the deal'. Everything else was lined up. It would have made Sheffield United. My father joked with the chairman, 'We won't need supporters - we'll have enough scouts watching Sheffield United'. But my father moved on and signed Alex Sabella as a replacement."

Sheffield United paid £160,000 for Sabella - just £40,000 less than the fee Haslam agreed to pay Argentinos Juniors for Maradona. Sabella impressed at Bramall Lane but could not prevent relegation into the Third Division at the end of the 1978-79 season and he was sold on to Leeds the following year for £400,000 while United dropped down again into the fourth tier. Meanwhile Maradona stayed at Argentinos Juniors until 1981, scoring 115 goals in 167 appearances, before joining Boca Juniors for around £2million and a year later he signed for Barcelona for a world-record fee of £5m and the rest, as they say, is history.

Keith Haslam was back in Argentina with his father four years later when Argentina played Czechoslovakia in a friendly at Mar del Plata in March 1982 and admitted he was mesmerised, "I've never seen anything like it," he said. "We met him in a restaurant at that time and everyone stood up to applaud him when he walked in. He was a god out there."

It was at this point that his father brokered a deal for a prospective move to Arsenal but circumstances would intervene. "[By this time] my dad had left Sheffield United and got a call from Terry Neill, the manager of Arsenal at the time, to see if he could broker a deal for Diego, knowing what had happened in '78. Again, a deal was negotiated in Buenos Aires for [Diego] to become an Arsenal player. The finances were all sorted out from the sponsor. Everything seemed fine when my dad came home from Buenos Aires but four days later Maggie Thatcher sent the fleet out to the Falklands and everything was scuppered. His agent at the time wanted him to come to England. His commercial value would have doubled." However, Neill's ultra ambitious plans to recruit some of the world's finest players were actually scuppered by his then blinkered board – Neill would be amazed that under a foreign coach Arsene Wenger Arsenal became the first club to play an entire foreign team!

THE SHIRT

Pele's iconic 1970 No 10 fetched a record £157,750 in 2002. Geoff Hurst's World Cup winning '66 hat-trick shirt fetched £91,750, but there was one shirt that had the potential to fetch a record that would never be beaten; £1 million for the No 10 blue Argentine shirt worn by Diego Maradona when he scored two of the World Cup's most prominent goals, the Hand of God goal followed by the 'Goal of the Century'.

This shirt is in a different hemisphere to any shirt sold at auction previously, simply because of the enormity of the personal performance of Maradona, both the Hand of God goal which is the most talked about World Cup goal, and his second against England which is the second most talked about goal and arguably the best ever in World Cup history. I have a collection of shirts at home, from Pelé to David Beckham, but this No10 shirt would without doubt be the most valuable shirt in the history of football.

I was there in the Azteca and I know how angry the England players were at the time, and understandably so, and some haven't got over it even to this day. Because of the frustration, disappointment, anger, none of the players thought about swapping shirts, none of them thought about asking for Diego's shirt except one player – Steve Hodge.

Peter Reid roomed with Hodge, and while there was fury that one of his team-mates had acquired the shirt of Diego Maradona, no one would be doubting the wisdom of acquiring the shirt under the current circumstances. It's value has soared as a result of Diego's death, as Reid told me: "Back in the dressing room there was quite a bit of anger, Butch (the late Ray Wilkins) had a go, Butch (Terry Butcher) and myself were not happy. Maradona was a great player, but he cheated for the first goal, and we all felt bitter disappointment in that dressing room, and I still feel like the now. However, we all witnessed a genius at work, the best player who ever walked this planet.

"Back at the team hotel, where I roomed with Steve Hodge,

I was lying on the bed, when Steve went to his kit bag and got it out. The shirt. You can imagine what I said to him. I couldn't imagine anyone going into that Argentine dressing room, let along asking for that shirt. It was the first time, back in that room, that I saw Steve with that blue No 10 shirt, and really I couldn't believe he had done it.

"Obviously I wouldn't have - I couldn't get anywhere near him throughout the game! When he got that brilliant second, he turned away from me and Peter Beardsley when he set off to score that wonderful goal, with that tremendous pace, and wonderful balance, which he showed on that day, but also in the semi-final against Belgium where he was man marked but it still didn't make any difference, as he tore them apart and he was again the best player in the Final. We thought about man marking him, but decided not to because he would wander all over the pitch, it was felt best to keep the shape of our own team. The Belgians man marked him with a specialist man marker they had in their team, but it made no difference, he still ran rings around them all."

Reid says he told Hodge "to go away in Anglo-Saxon. As for that shirt, well, I might have gone ballistic when I saw it, but Steve isn't such a mug now as that shirt must be worth a small fortune. Dear me, I would hate to put a price on it. "Is it worth £1million? I have no idea, I couldn't put a price on it and I'm not sure anyone could, it would be worth an amazing amount now."

The shirt swap happened because Hodge was delayed leaving the pitch by an ITV interview. "I was walking down the tunnel and Maradona was coming in the opposite direction. I just tugged my shirt and we swapped there and then. I have no idea if he still has mine." Hodge's backpass was at the heart of Maradona punching his mistake past Peter Shilton for the "Hand of God" goal on 50 minutes. He is also the owner of the Argentinian captain's No 10 shirt from that day even entitling his autobiography *The Man With Maradona's Shirt*. Hodge is always asked whether his pass back to Shilton was intended. "I tell them that it was, I hit it with my strong left foot on the right side of the ball with the intention that it would spin back. It was a slice but it was an intended slice. I just thought that the goalkeeper would pick it up and we would squeeze up. For his second goal you can see me on the footage just two or three yards behind him after he is challenged on the halfway line at the start of his run. I thought I would tuck in and get back and that someone would hold him up and we could regroup. But you could see he was getting at the back four too easily and then it was down to the goalkeeper. The dummy he sold Shilton was brilliant."

I had a call from someone who wanted to track down the shirt a couple of years ago, willing to pay £300,000. I contacted Steve Hodge who told me he wasn't interested in selling at that time, and wouldn't even consider it at that price, that it was far too low and he had been offered more and rejected it. Clearly he thought it would be worth at least twice or even three times as much at some point in time – and that point has now arrived.

The shirt was one of the most popular artefacts in the National Football Museum in Manchester, loaned to them for exhibitions since 2003. "To have a Diego Maradona shirt on display would be amazing in itself but to have 'the' shirt, the one he wore on June 22, 1986 and scored those two goals, for us, is absolutely phenomenal," said Dickie Felton, spokesperson for the National Football Museum, told PA news agency. "Our visitors, they love it. It provokes so many talking points because it is 'the' shirt and it provokes so many memories of people watching the game all those years ago.

"We were very lucky and fortunate in that Steve Hodge loaned us this remarkable piece of football history. So many thousands of visitors have seen it over the years. It is an astonishing artefact. I am in this museum all the time but when I walk past it I have to stop and look at it because of what it is. It almost has a certain power to it, still. It is quite something to have it on display here in Manchester."

The story of Hodge acquiring the shirt resurfaced following Diego's passing. As for its value now, that remains a matter of conjecture. Felton said: "We would never put a monetary figure on objects and items but the cultural value of this is absolutely immense. I think, after 34 years, England fans have got over the heartbreak now and I think Maradona will be completely remembered for that second goal. The first one, the 'Hand of God', will disappear and it will be all about that second goal where he took on several players. It was poetry in motion. It was art, it was opera, it was remarkable. I think it was the greatest goal ever seen."

Hodge declared that Maradona's iconic shirt is not for sale, even for £1 million, after an "uncomfortable" week following the iconic stars death fending off calls and dealing with "disrespectful" rumours that he was trying to hawk around the shirt to the highest bidder.

Talking for the first time since Maradona's tragic death, Hodge told BBC Radio Nottingham, "I have had it for 34 years and have never once tried to sell it," "I like having it. It has incredible sentimental value."

But Hodge, now 58, has been perturbed by false rumours that he has actually been actively trying to find a buyer. He explained: "I've had people knocking on my door non-stop and the phone's constantly ringing from every TV and radio station, and even foreign stations. It has been uncomfortable and it hasn't been nice. I have seen articles on the internet and there has been a bit of flak flying around saying I wanted a million or two million and am hawking it around for money. I find it disrespectful and totally wrong. It's not for sale. I am not trying to sell it."

For the time being, the Maradona Shirt is on display at the National Football Museum in Manchester. "One day in the future one never knows," Hodge added. "But I have never once tried to sell it, and definitely not at the moment. "If you ever want to go and see it, it's in Manchester."

Hodge, who played for Nottingham Forest for a total of eight years over two spells, as well as Aston Villa, Tottenham and Leeds

United, now works as a pundit and is a regular co-commentator on BBC Radio Nottingham. He had a close-up view of the sinner and saint, the villain and the hero all in one intoxicating mix, all in that one game, that defined the Argentine legend, but also defined the career of so many others including Hodge, because he was the one who ended up with the shirt his team-mates turned their noses up at.

Hodge now says: "Yes, he hurt us in 1986 and that will always be there but from every corner of the globe he was respected and people appreciated the genius he had. That game will never be forgotten in the history of football. I have to say I have never once blamed him for the handball. Not once. It was out of order but people who play football know that you try things now and again. It was a big-pressure match and he took a risk. Thierry Henry did a handball a few years ago and got away with that one. On big occasions when the stakes are high - and this was monstrously high having had a war four years before that - he took a gamble."

The defining moment in Hodges' career is that he played the ball up in the air towards keeper Peter Shilton.

"It was flicked back, it wasn't sliced horribly. I caught it perfectly," Hodge recalled "and I turned around thinking Peter could come out and catch the ball, but he [Maradona] appeared from nowhere. A striker will normally slow down with a big keeper coming out thinking he might get hurt, but he didn't. The bravery to take on a 6ft 1ins keeper when he was 5ft 5ins showed he didn't give a damn. He was as brave as a lion. He used to get kicked to ribbons everywhere he played."

No-one, Hodge included, could stop Maradona on the way to scoring the 'goal of the century'. "And I had the privilege of being five yards behind him all the way for the second goal" he added, "what a player. He was just a genius.

"People say to me, 'why didn't you sprint back?' Well, it was an hour gone and if you are several thousand feet above sea level and you have made a run forward, trust me, you cannot get back. There was no air in my lungs."

The game in Mexico was the second time Hodge had the "pleasure" of sharing a pitch with Maradona. The first was with Forest in 1983 during pre-season when the two-time European Cup champions faced Barcelona at the Nou Camp, played after a "proper downpour". Hodge said: "The game was basically played in a quagmire. They couldn't cancel it because there were already 100,000 people in the stadium. We were a good team then and were always top two or three in the First Division and when you saw someone like that come along you just realised , 'wow, this guy is from another planet'. Players wouldn't normally try to dribble the ball through the water but he was flicking the ball up with his left foot, not once or twice but two, three, or four times, looking up and volleying it around the Nou Camp. His ball mastery was just incredible. For a kid like me, who was 21 at the time, I thought I was useful but this guy is far more useful than me. It was a reality check."

1986 AND ALL THAT

In the days following Maradona's passing, the BBC broadcast a re-run of the 1986 World Cup quarter-final played in front of 115,000 fans at the Estadio Azteca in Mexico City on Sunday 22 June 1986 and treated it as if it were being reported today, with video, pictures, interaction, even twitter. It was a brilliant, notorious performance from Diego Maradona, encapsulating everything about him – as both Saint and Sinner all within this one game. It was the game to which he will always be most closely associated, more so in England than anywhere else in the world.

The BBC made it possible to experience it again, or enjoy it for the first time. A few days after Maradona's death, the BBC had the game available across all their platforms to honour the Argentina great. It was also accompanied by live text commentary on the BBC Sport website for the public to share their thoughts on the classic game and join the conversation.

Taking us back in time the on line coverage began with: "Here we go, this is the one we've all been waiting for. Grab a cuppa, turn Wham! off the wireless and bag yourself a decent spot on the sofa – it's England versus Argentina in a World Cup quarter-final."

I was there in Mexico for the *Daily Mirror* and watched England's final training session standing on the edge of the pitch, which had been transformed from its usual use – the local bullring. In those days, the much smaller press corps were allowed far greater access to the players and the training sessions. The 1986 World Cup began for England some distance from Mexico City high in the mountainous region of Monterrey. The training camp, though, was in Mexico City in a lovely area belonging to the cricket club where the majority of English ex-pats lived in desirable properties, all open plan and very smart even back in those days. A daily convoy would set off from the England camp's lavish accommodation, in a sparkling complex, to make the half an hour journey. The convoy was necessary because we were billeted in bandit country. There were armed guards on the England team coaches, while the media travelled behind in hired cars, they needed the protection to make sure they made it to training without being kidnapped which was a specialism of the bandits. Bobby Robson would hold his media briefings in the picturesque grounds of the hotel. The new Spurs manager David Pleat, working as a pundit, was staying there along with the TV commentators and crew.

England's opponents for their opening group game, Portugal, were staying just 500 yards over the road, which made it hugely convenient to nip over to their media briefings. Their team had been on strike for a week leading up to the opening game arguing over unfulfilled promises of bonus payments and expenses. The Portuguese FA finally relented just 72 hours before their opening game with England, and they managed only a couple of training sessions so, we presumed it would be a walkover, but it proved anything but on a diabolical pitch in a ridiculously poor stadium for a World Cup group game. Against Morocco in the second game things got even worse as talisman and skipper Bryan Robson injured his shoulder again and Ray Wilkins was dismissed a minute later for throwing the ball to the ground in frustration in the direction of the referee. After hanging on for a goalless draw it looked like an uphill battle to make it out of the group stage but fortunately England finally found their form against Poland in the final game, racing into a 3 goal lead within half an hour thanks to a Gary Lineker hat trick and the second phase of the tournament would see the team based in the capital

So as I stood on the periphery of the training session before the Argentina game Don Howe, Bobby Robson's trusted coach, with whom I had a long and close professional relationship, confided in me that there has been a long and hard debate within the camp whether to man mark Maradona. Howe was a hugely influential defensive coach and it was his recommendation that Maradona needed to be closely shadowed throughout the game. Howe also confided in me that had skipper Bryan Robson been fit then he would be the man to man mark Maradona. Robson came into the tournament with a worrying shoulder injury which he injured in the final group game in Monterrey. He was back in the team hotel continuing his rehabilitation, as he stayed on in the hope he would be fit for the later stages should England go deep into the tournament. From Howe's perspective Captain Marvel was not totally fit but fit enough to man mark Maradona, rather than rampage up and down the pitch as usual.

After that training session I rushed back as quickly as I could, which wasn't easy, through the rush hour traffic in Mexico City, to get to my hotel as quickly as I could to 'file' the big story that England had been thinking of man marking Maradona with the injured Bryan Robson. Given the time difference, the story only made the final editions of the *Daily Mirror*.

As it turned out, Bobby Robson thought about it again over night, but opted to play safe and persevere with the fully fit Peter Reid, and not to indulge Maradona with a man marker, as both the England manager and Howe, both agreed on one thing, that Bryan Robson was the only man capable of doing that job effectively.

Peter Reid now tells me, "The position in midfield was between myself and Bryan Robson, but Robbo was not fully fit and I am still not convinced that man marking Maradona would have worked. Belgium tried it with one of the best specialist man markers in the world and Maradona still ran rings around them in the semi-finals, he tore Belgium apart and was man of the match again in the Final, there was just no stopping him at this time, he was at the height of his powers.

"Yes, I can remember that we did talk about man marking him, we did have that discussion, and I think had Bryan been fully fit, maybe Bobby would have done it, but to this day I am not sure anyone could have stopped Maradona."

I reminded Peter Reid how successfully Alan Mullery had man-marked Pelé in Mexico in 1970, but he laughed: "Yes, he did, but England still lost!" He added: "Also with the greatest respect to Pelé, he played in a formidable Brazil team in the 70s."

However, Maradona was very much virtually a one-man show, and it will always remain with me just how close Bobby Robson came to bringing Bryan Robson out of the pool and into the deep end with a man to man marking job on Maradona, and how maybe that might have changed the course of history. Not much was made of that prospect at the time, and it isn't mentioned much now. Later that day, when Maradona produced his phenomenal display to knock out England, I was the only journalist to ask the England manager whether he regretted not man marking Maradona, and he was honest enough to tell me that he did.

Before the game, Bobby Moore, speaking in the *Sunday Telegraph* said, "I've not seen anyone so far in these finals who would be capable of marking Diego Maradona on a man-to-man basis. To do that, you've got to be as quick, strong and mobile as he is. It's impossible to make comparisons with other great players, but the one Diego Maradona reminds me of most is Johan Cruyff. He had the same fluency on the ball and could damage you from nothing. But he didn't have Maradona's incredible strength. Pelé was the most complete footballer I ever saw, he could have played in any position and done well. Maradona is not his equal in the air and is more one-footed, but he does have the same deep, instinctive understanding of how to inflict the greatest damage in any attacking situation."

Bobby Robson made only one change that day, though, he brought back QPR's central defender Terry Fenwick after serving his one-match suspension, replacing Alvin Martin to once again partner Ipswich's Terry Butcher. Up front, Peter Beardsley kept his place alongside the revelation of the tournament, Gary Lineker. Lineker was level at the top of the Golden Boot standings with Spain forward Emilio Butragueño and Brazil's Careca; all three on five goals.

Lineker had been on fire and was England's big hope and had been the man of the tournament, so far, along with Michael

Laudrup who had inspired Denmark, arguably the most exciting team of the tournament, living up to their "Danish Dynamite" tag before their implosion in the second round losing 5-1 to Spain with Emilio Butragueño scoring four!

Diego Maradona was also in sensational form, leaving defenders for dead with his near-perfect mix of touch, strength, pace, power and precision and because of his hero worship status with Napoli and adoration throughout Italy, the Italians suffered mixed emotions as many supported Maradona as much, if not more in some regions, ahead of Italy. After an injury-hit spell in Barcelona, he had reinvented himself at Napoli. Yet while Maradona had plenty of 'assists' to his name, prior to the England game, though, he had only actually only scored once, and had been over shadowed by the goalscoring prowess of the Barcelona bound Lineker, whose five goals, averaging a goal every 71.2 minutes in the tournament.

For all his faults, England manager Bobby Robson was loved by his players; he was a passionate man who wanted nothing more than to lead his country to glory. Before the game he said: "I had a bit of success at Ipswich, that was parochial, that was for the people of Suffolk, it was warm and smashing. This is for the country, it means so much more. It is for the people of Manchester, Plymouth, Carlisle, wherever they watch football because everyone loves it, no more than us."

As a result the England camp I had been observing so closely on a day to day basis were in confident mood. Big Terry Butcher summed up their bullish attitude before the quarter-final, "We're all looking forward to it. It's the biggest game I've ever played in. My hair is getting too long now, I don't want to cut it until we lose. Hopefully that won't be today…"

It was rumoured at the time that Argentina coach Carlos

Bilardo was concerned about the soaring temperatures for this midday kick-off in Mexico City, so asked the Argentine kit manufacturer to come up with new shirts at short notice. According to FIFA, he sent a member of his coaching staff to the shops in the Mexican capital to find new ones. He returned with two, and Maradona had the final say on the one Argentina wore. Makeshift Argentinian Football Association badges were quickly sewn on to each jersey and numbers ironed on the back.

The nation was a bag of nerves, and so too was the injured skipper, as Bryan Robson observed at the time, "When you're on the bench, you are seeing everything and every time the opposition gets in the box, you think 'here we go'. I think we will beat them. From what I have seen in the World Cup so far, there is nothing we should be frightened of. Okay, they have Diego Maradona and Jorge Valdano, but if we do well against them, we will do well in the game."

Yet Jimmy Hill's comments on the BBC proved to be a portent, "the conversation over coffee this morning was about the poor quality of refereeing in the tournament and most journalists around the world agree with that. They use the inexperienced referees or those from emerging countries in the vital games.

It was a sweltering hot day in the Azteca Stadium, and I turned up in shorts, not the usual attire for the press box, but on this day, I think everyone in the press box was in shorts.

Re-watching the game 34 years later it's incredible how much attention England paid to Maradona. The first time he was able to turn and run at the England defence, Terry Fenwick brings him down and the QPR man is shown a yellow card which would prove pivotal later as Fenwick would later recall how he thought about bringing Maradona down when he went on his run for his second goal, but pulled out knowing he would have received a red card.

BBC commentator Barry Davies then observed "That's the first we've seen of the little man. And, great player that he is, it would be best if we don't see much more of him…So far - and

I hope I'm not tempting fate - England have been able to crowd Diego Maradona out…

Jimmy Hill observed "If England are going to win this game, goalkeeper Peter Shilton, the captain, will have an opportunity to prove he is the best. He has a lot more work to do yet. Not an easy task for England when Diego Maradona is in possession. Of a disappointing goalless first half, Barry Davies observed, "I think it is fair to say that only Maradona has looked like making a breakthrough, he's the only one who's committed players in the last third of the field.

During half-time then Barcelona manager Terry Venables criticised England's approach, "We don't know what England have been sent out to do, they are showing the opposition so much respect. Glenn Hoddle is defending with the rest, we need to risk him and leave him up the pitch so Argentina will worry about him.

Former England captain Emlyn Hughes added, "Diego Maradona has done well and we all know how good he is. Bobby Robson has a major part to play now at half-time. It hasn't been a great game but he needs to go in and tell them 'Ey, we have a chance.' We can push Glenn Hoddle further forward and if he can start playing and putting the ball to the front players, we can do well. Argentina are nothing special.

The second half began in a similar vein to the first but then, on 51 minutes, came the moment that fixes the player and the game in English minds. Maradona sets off on a jinking run towards the England penalty box, shifts it right to Jorge Valdano and it loops back into his path off the boot of Steve Hodge. Somehow, the 5ft 5in Maradona out leaped England goalkeeper Peter Shilton to help it into an empty net. Maradona sprints off to celebrate and beckons his team-mates to join him.

Barry Davies: "England are appealing for offside but the goal is given. Or was it the use of the hand that England are appealing against? Maradona's arm was up…"but as Ossie Ardiles said in his introduction to this book, Maradona anticipated the backpass, and that's why he kept on running.

The England players surround Tunisian referee Ali Bin Naser as Peter Shilton and Terry Fenwick point to their hands. The BBC replays showed a clear handball. Surely FIFA need to bring in VAR sooner rather than later? Well, 34 years later!

England have still not recovered from that first set back when, four minutes later, Maradona scores the FIFA 'Goal of the Century' As Glenn Hoddle pointed out earlier in this book, he felt there was a foul on him before the ball spun to Maradona, although Hoddle thinks it was a close decision on whether a foul would have been given if there had been VAR. Maradona collected the ball five yards inside the England half, facing the opposition goal, accelerating away from Peter Reid, waltzes inside Terry Butcher and then eases beyond Terry Fenwick into the penalty area. Maradona shaped to shoot but instead rolled the ball past the onrushing Peter Shilton and slides his effort into an empty net, despite Butcher's last-ditch attempts to tackle him.

Maradona 2, England 0.

It was a goal that brought a magnanimous piece of commentary from Barry Davies "You have to say that's magnificent! There is no doubt about that goal. Pure football genius. If the first was illegal, the second was one of the best we've seen in this championship. The crowd in the Azteca stand to Maradona."

In contrast Argentinian commentator Victor Hugo Morales described the goal as follow "Maradona has the ball, two mark him, he touches the ball. The genius of world football dashes to the right and leaves the third and is going to pass to Burruchaga. It's still Maradona! Genius! Genius! Genius! Ta-ta-ta-ta-ta-ta-ta. Gooooooooooal! Gooooooooooal! I want to cry! Dear God! Long live football! Gooooooooooal! Diegoal! Maradona! It's enough to make you cry, forgive me. Maradona, in an unforgettable run, in the play of all time. Cosmic kite! What planet are you from? Leaving in your wake so many Englishmen, so that the whole country is a clenched fist shouting for Argentina? Argentina 2, England 0. Diegoal, Diegoal, Diego Armando Maradona. Thank you, God, for football, for Maradona, for these tears, for this, Argentina 2, England 0.

A stunned Jimmy Hill in awe at what he's just seen "When we look at our own players back home, some of them being sold expensively to Italy, I think in all honesty we can say there is no light that shines as brightly as Maradona. He can do it on his own, he can lay it on for other people; can take part in inter-passing movements, has fantastic pace, also tremendous strength; he's won a couple of headers in midfield and on that fine one, unfair or not, he still read the backpass quicker than Shilton did and the ball was running away from him."

Peter Reid gets another kick, this one from Sergio Baptista, the Everton man is seething and Baptista goes into the book. John Barnes and Chris Waddle are warming up. Reid, who had a knock before the game and took a few more during it, is replaced by Waddle as Bobby Robson looks to gamble.

After the second goal Glenn Hoddle springs into life in this contest, firing a free-kick around the wall which forces goalkeeper Nery Pumpido into a diving one-handed save.

Jimmy Hill, "The game was altered by an unfair decision or non recognition, but otherwise Argentina have played with more imagination, attacked more and deserve to be in the lead."

John Barnes comes on for Trevor Steven and on 81 minutes Gary Linker pulls England back into the contest from Barnes' floated cross. The Watford winger wriggles down the left and picks out his prolific centre forward, who heads beyond Argentina goalkeeper Nery Pumpido from inside the six-yard box. It was enough to win Lineker the Golden Boot, but did it come too late for England?

In the closing stages Maradona is back defending, taking the ball from Waddle, and then in the 88th minute another bad referring decision, or rather lack of a decision. Lineker was inches away from levelling the score. Great work from Barnes again on England's left, picking out Lineker at the back post with a superb cross, but the striker can't quite get his head to it as he is pushed over and into the net. It's a clear foul, a clear penalty.

England had finally woken up in the final 15 minutes of the game and should have had an equaliser. If only they'd been a little bit more attack-minded at 0-0! But it was Argentina who made into the World Cup semi-finals, and all because of one man: Diego Armando Maradona.

Back in the studio the inquest begins – Terry Venables "For the first goal, Peter Shilton should have come out and clattered the man and the ball. He was slow off his line. You can't blame the linesman as I thought Diego Maradona headed the ball. His hand was up but it looked like a header.

England left-back on the day Kenny Sansom later remarked, "Nobody talked to Diego Maradona after the game – we wouldn't go near him. Steve Hodge got his shirt after the game and when he came into the dressing room we gave him loads of abuse about it. Now it's worth £250,000 so I wish I got it! But there was a lot of anger in the dressing room. Three or four men from the FA came in and we were asking them to get the game replayed, saying it was a disgrace. They were just as gutted as we were but there was nothing that they could do."

Maradona, talking to BBC Match of the Day presenter Gary Lineker in 2006, admitted "It was my hand. I don't mean any disrespect to English fans but this is something that happens. I scored goals before in Argentina with my hands. It was a ball that I couldn't reach, Peter Shilton was already there, I couldn't head it so I moved my head back [and used my hand]. I started running and Shilton didn't see what I had done. The sweeper told him as he is the one who saw my hand. When I saw the linesman running, I shouted 'goal' and I looked behind to see whether the referee had taken the bait and he had so that was it. Come on, come on, it was a goal!"

Argentinians saw the match as revenge for their country's loss to Britain in the 1982 Falkland war, which they still claim as "Las Malvinas." "It was our way of recovering 'Las Malvinas,'" Maradona wrote in his 2000 autobiography *I am Diego*, "it was more than trying to win a game. We said the game had nothing to do with the war. But we knew that Argentines had died there, that they had killed them like birds. And this was our revenge. It was something bigger than us: We were defending our flag." Ahead of his 60th birthday in October, Maradona told *France Football* magazine that it was his dream to "score another goal against the English, this time with the right hand."

The Tunisian referee later claimed he was "proud and honoured" to have helped Diego Maradona score the 'Goal of the Century" when he beat several England players on a mazy dribble from just inside his own half before scoring to put Argentina 2-0 up, four minutes after scoring the controversial "Hand of God" goal. Referee Ali Bin Nasser, now 76, insists he had no option but to award the first goal and recalled how Maradona gave him a signed shirt when they met again in 2015.

Of the second goal, Bin Nasser told BBC Sport, "He took off from midfield, and I was shadowing him closely. When you're refereeing someone like Maradona, you can't take your eyes off them. They tried to take him down on three occasions, but his desire for victory kept pushing him forward. Every time I would shout 'advantage' until he reached the box. I was watching from outside the box, wondering how this player shook off three defenders, and sprinted for nearly 50 metres. I thought 'the defenders will try to take him down now'. I was expecting that to happen and was ready to whistle for a penalty. To my surprise, he dribbled past another defender and the goalkeeper to score what would become 'the goal of the century'. I'm proud and honoured as a person and as a referee for having played a role in that historical achievement. Had I whistled [for] a foul in any of the first three contacts, we wouldn't have witnessed something that magnificent. That advantage I gave is one my proudest achievements."

Bin Nasser added that was the "highlight" of his career, despite his decision to the controversial first goal. "I remember it vividly. The English defender had the ball, sent it back and Maradona was in the air with Peter Shilton, and they were both facing away from me. They were facing my assistant referee, the Bulgarian Bogdan Dochev. I was hesitant at first, I glanced over to Dochev, who was headed back to the centre of the pitch, confirming the goal. He didn't signal for handball. The instructions FIFA gave us before the game were clear – if a colleague was in a better position than mine, I should respect his view."

Dochev, who died in 2017 aged 80 said that "FIFA did not allow assistants to discuss decisions with the referee. If FIFA had put a referee from Europe in charge of such an important game, the first goal of Maradona would have been disallowed," he insisted.

Bin Nasser says the sportsmanship shown by the England players was "beautiful". He recalled: "Gary Lineker came over to me and said 'please referee, handball!' I replied: Please play!' To me, that was 100% a goal according to FIFA guidelines."

But all was not lost as England pulled one back and then besieged the Argentina goal with Lineker coming close to an equaliser. "When England scored their goal, I secretly wanted them to score the equaliser," admitted Bin Nasser. "I wanted to enjoy that game for 30 more minutes. It was an absolute joy from start to finish. Despite the heat that day, I wanted things to go on. It was a beautiful game between two great teams." So why did he not give the penalty right at the end for a clear foul?

When Maradona came to Tunisia in 2015, he visited Bin Nasser at his home. "I told him 'it wasn't Argentina that won the World Cup that year, it was Maradona'. He replied: 'Had it not been for you, I wouldn't have been able to score the goal of the century.' He gave me a signed jersey that said 'Para Ali Mi Amigo Eterna.'"

The contrast between England and Argentina couldn't have been greater in Mexico – for England five-star accommodation at the Cameo Real hotel, for Argentina a humble B&B. In fact so poor was the accommodation that the world's greatest player decided to decorate the walls of his room with posters of the Virgin Mary and Argentine singer Valeria Lynch, partly in an attempt to cover the exposed brickwork in their shabby hotel room. Maradona described Argentina's accommodation as a 'whorehouse without the whores' but it engendered team spirit as they plotted their World Cup triumph during four weeks there. Pedro Pasculli's part in Argentina's success was negligible on the field, off it, as company for Diego, it proved to be vitally important. In that shabby room, on the night of Argentina's 2-1 victory over England in the quarter-final, they watched highlights of the game.

"'The Hand of God was a craftiness," Pasculli recalls from his home in the Italian city of Lecce, where he played between 1985 and 1992. "In Italy we would call it *furbizia* (cunning). Only a champion like Diego could do that. But then, he made everything good with the best goal in World Cup history, and maybe the greatest goal ever. It was a sensational goal… crazy. We watched the goals again together. We joked about the craftiness of the first. Many players have tried that sort of thing and failed, but he succeeded at a World Cup - that is Diego."

Pasculli had been a team-mate of Maradona with Argentinos Juniors and won a move to Serie A after scoring more than 100 goals in his homeland. So when there was a split in the camp on the eve of the tournament - one half behind 1978 World Cup-winning captain Daniel Passarella, the other with Maradona - Pasculli inevitably sided with Diego, despite being labelled a 'rebel' by Passarella. "We weren't rebels. It was like any family, it happens, there was a problem inside the team. All of the players had a meeting, and we resolved it." Maradona resolved it calling Passarella a 'backstabber' and accusing him of being responsible for an unpaid phone bill which, because no-one had confessed to, was to be split between the squad.

Finally, all the players rallied behind Maradona. Days later

Passarella withdrew because of a calf strain. Maradona was the new captain. 'Then,' Pasculli added, 'we won the World Cup. We won because the team was strong, we were close-knit.'

In those days the media corps stayed with the players, I knew that they enjoyed lavish facilities. The complex even boasted a huge disco, which some of the media enjoyed, even David Pleat was spotted there from time to time, although the players mainly stayed within their own section.

But due to the chronic lack of amenities at Argentina's B&B, the players would loosen the screws of the masseur's bed for entertainment and watch through a window as he crashed to the floor. "We got out and relaxed - we went to the shopping mall, walked around and ate hot dogs and ice-cream," said Pasculli, "afterwards, we ate at a steak restaurant, all of the team and staff together. We then joined a group of Argentine supporters and celebrated our win, singing with them."

Visits to Helen's Ice-Cream parlour and the steakhouse became team rituals. Bonnie Tyler's hit *Total Eclipse of the Heart* and the *Rocky* soundtrack were played on the team bus and in the dressing-room, they became part of the ritual, that they had to perform if they wanted to continue in the tournament.

Argentina's opening group match saw a 3-1 win over South Korea. Before and after that game the squad believed they had found a winning formula, which became a superstition; escaping the team hotel. Pasculli started alongside Maradona for the last-16 tie against Uruguay. As Scotland had discovered in the group stages their South American rivals had only one tactic - kick anything that moved, especially Maradona! "They were a rough, aggressive and ferocious team," said Pasculli. "Diego was a special player, so they marked him, man-to-man." Just before half-time, with the game goalless, Argentina broke upfield. "Diego dribbled and passed to Sergio Batista," recalled Pasculli, "the defender anticipated his movement and the ball ran to Jorge Burruchaga. He passed to Jorge Valdano who played the ball towards me. I had only the goalkeeper to beat. I looked him in the eye and placed it to his left. Goal. It was 56 years since Argentina had won a South American derby at the World Cup, and my goal had done it, that was an incredible feeling."

When Argentina played England at the Azteca Stadium in Mexico City for a place in the semi-final, Pasculli expected to start. Then, the night before the game, coach Carlos Bilardo knocked at No 6 and asked Maradona for a word outside. The captain was there when Bilardo broke the news that his friend would not play. Maradona later wrote in his book, 'Touched by God', that Pasculli 'cried like a baby', but later he said: 'I did not cry. I was unhappy because I had played well and scored the winning goal. But the coach always thought of the opponent when he picked the team and I respected that. Myself and Diego talked. He is a champion, he knew how to give peace and the right advice.'

Maradona insisted the players could not wear their alternative blue jersey against England in the midday heat – at altitude – because it was too thick. Bilardo used a pair of scissors to pierce holes in the shirts in an attempt to keep the players happy. It did not work. 'We could not wear those jerseys, so it was a race against the clock,' explained Pasculli. 'One of the directors had to go into the city to look for new shirts. Eventually, the day before the game, we found some.' Two seamstresses were drafted in to sew on the numbers and national emblem. The emergency tailoring worked and in the semi-final a few days later Maradona continued to dominate the tournament with both goals in a 2-0 victory over Belgium.

For the final against West Germany, the night before, Maradona turned to Pasculli as neither of them could sleep, and they needed to take their minds off the momentous occasion that would confront them. In the darkness, they went for a walk. "Playing a World Cup final is not easy," said Pasculli "you feel so much pressure, it was a wait that never ended, it is very difficult to sleep. You can imagine the pressure of a decisive game to win Serie A or the Premier League but for this final, it was 1,000 per cent more. But for Diego, that emotion was normal. With Diego near you, everything is easier. He talked to me all night, this allowed me to temper myself. Having Diego as a team-mate represented for us all the guarantee that, in the end, we would win the World Cup."

A topsy-turvy final saw Argentina go two goals ahead before the Germans levelled matters, scoring twice in 5 minutes. Then, with just minutes to go, Maradona produced a sublime turn and pass to release Burruchaga for the winner. At the final whistle there is a famous picture of Maradona on the shoulders of a fan as he holds the trophy aloft. Next to him, also being hoisted in the air, is Pasculli. "There are no words to describe it," he said, "you have to live it to understand. You lift that trophy and show it to the whole world - you are the winner!"

The squad flew back to Buenos Aires that same evening, but not before returning to their squalid base. "We kept a promise to ourselves and placed the trophy on the grass of the training pitch," commented Pasculli. "We then did a victory lap around the field, just us, hugging each other and celebrating. It was a special moment." Back in their room, Pasculli and Maradona drank Chivas Regal whisky and the party continued on their flight home, where a hero's reception awaited at the palace in Plaza de Mayo. "Physically, that flight was like playing another game," says Pasculli, "dancing, singing, drinking. But to bring that happiness to your countrymen… it is the most incredible feeling."

DIEGO IN HIS OWN WORDS, AND WHAT THEY SAID ABOUT HIM DOWN THE YEARS

"The crucial difference with Pele is that Maradona wasn't surrounded by great players; he had to carry the team himself. If you took Maradona out of Argentina, they would not win the World Cup, but I think Brazil without Pele would still have won." — Eric Cantona.

"To see the ball, to run after it, makes me the happiest man in the world."

"I made mistakes, and I paid for them. But the ball is still pure — Speaking to the crowd at his 2001 testimonial."

"I am Maradona, who makes goals, who makes mistakes. I can take it all, I have shoulders big enough to fight with everybody."

"You can say a lot of things about me, but you can never say I don't take risks."

"I am black or white, I'll never be grey in my life."

"When I wear the national team shirt, its contact with my skin makes it stand on an end."

"I hate everything that comes from the United States. I hate it with all my strength."

"Suck it, and keep sucking it!"— To journalists who had doubted him as Argentina coach.

On Pelé

"There would be no debate about who was the best footballer the world had ever seen, me or Pelé. Everyone would say me."

"Pelé should go back to the museum."

On the Hand of God

"I was waiting for my team-mates to embrace me and no one came... I told them, 'Come hug me or the referee isn't going to allow it'."

"If I could apologise and go back and change history I would do. But the goal is still a goal, Argentina became world champions and I was the best player in the world."

On Lionel Messi

"Messi scores a goal and celebrates. Cristiano (Ronaldo) scores a goal and poses like he's in a shampoo commercial."

What they said about Diego Maradona

"Even if I played for a million years, I'd never come close to Maradona. Not that I'd want to anyway. He's the greatest there's ever been" Lionel Messi.

"No ball ever had a better experience than when it was at his left foot." — Argentina team-mate Jorge Valdano.

"Diego, for all Argentinians, is God. And he always will be." Carlos Tevez.

"What Zidane could do with a ball, Maradona could do with an orange." Michel Platini.

"The best of the lot, no question… I saw Maradona do things that God himself would doubt were possible." Zico.

"The best I ever played against was Maradona." Paolo Maldini.

"He was a model of good behaviour on the pitch. He was respectful of everyone, from the great players down to the ordinary team member. He was always getting kicked around and he never complained, not like some of today's strikers." Maldini.

"When he was on form, there was almost no way of stopping him Franco Baresi.

"The best player I've seen in my life. A genius." Marcel Desailly.

"The best player there has ever been, better than Pelé" Ruud Gullit.

"When Diego scored that second goal against us, I felt like applauding. I'd never felt like that before, but it's true… It was impossible to score such a beautiful goal. He's the greatest player of all time, by a long way." Gary Lineker.

"For Maradona to win a World Cup on his own, and let's face it, that's what he did as the rest of the team were ordinary, was an amazing achievement. He was the best player I've seen" Glenn Hoddle.

"The crucial difference with Pelé is that Maradona wasn't surrounded by great players; he had to carry the team himself. If you took Maradona out of Argentina, they would not win the World Cup, but I think Brazil without Pelé would still have won." Eric Cantona.

"He only wanted the ball. He wasn't about running; he was all about the game... It's difficult to explain exactly what he would do from the noise the ball would make when his foot connected with it to his incredible control and the swerve he could put on it." former team-mate Mauricio Pochettino.

"In Argentine football there is a before and after Maradona" — Julio Grondona, former head of the Argentine football association.

"What great sadness that Maradona has gone. He has gone too soon. He meant so much, even now, after his playing career." Lionel Messi, provided one of the most poignant tributes revealing the shirt of one of his former clubs, Newell's Old Boys, following his goal for Barcelona in the 4-0 win over Osasuna. Leeds manager Marcelo Bielsa, who both played for and managed Newell's, added "What a brilliant tribute from Messi, uniting Diego and Newell's."

"Diego, what planet are you from? I want to cry, oh holy God, long live football! What a goal!" Victor Hugo Morales' Argentinian TV commentary on the Goal of the Century against England.

"The comparison, of the two goals, I have always called the Finger of the Devil, rather than the Hand of God, they were four minutes apart. What I found to say, compared back to say, 'That was pure' because the other one was unquestionably cheating. It was extraordinary. When he received the ball he was in his own half of the centre circle, facing his own goal, and turned and went off on a run that cut the England defence to shreds. There were attempts to tackle him but somehow he wasn't there. He could have passed the ball but had no intention of doing anything other than scoring. In England he's remembered for Beauty and the Beast, or it should be Beast and the Beauty, that way around." Barry Davies.

MARADONA TALES...

Gary Lineker might not have covered himself in glory with his clever play on words when he posted one of his notorious tweets immediately hearing the death of Diego Maradona. But, in reality, Lineker had nothing but respect for Maradona, and even decided to embark on a meaningful documentary on the Argentine. As this book sets out to decide whether he was hero or villain, those who knew him best considered him more hero than villain.

Lineker got the opportunity to interview Maradona in 2016 to discuss his career on and off the pitch in detail for a BBC documentary. Lineker couldn't resist asking him which hand he used during a jokey exchange when first meeting Maradona. In the clip, Lineker is seen shaking hands with Maradona before asking him: "Which hand was it, this one?"

Maradona responds with a laugh and cheekily lifts his left arm up to Lineker, telling him while shaking his wrist: "No, it was this one!" Maradona was often asked about the Hand of God and he never ducked responsibility for it, showed any embarrassment for it, nor apologised for it.

He actually revelled in the controversy. "I knew it was my hand," said Maradona in 2019. "It wasn't my plan but the action happened so fast that the linesman didn't see me putting my hand in. The referee looked at me and he said: 'Goal.' It was a nice feeling like some sort of symbolic revenge against the English."

The documentary marked the 30th anniversary of Argentina's quarter-final against England, arguably Maradona's most iconic performance in a national team shirt. The programme reflected on the match, England's performances in the lead-up, and the game's political dimension four years after the Falklands War. It featured contributions from England greats who played including Lineker, Glenn Hoddle, Kenny Sansom, Terry Butcher, Steve Hodge and Peter Shilton. Produced by Lineker's own company Goalhanger Films, the documentary blended those insights from veteran players with archive material and music from the time for an insight into one of the most famous moments in the history of the game.

Lineker talks about Maradona with great affection and recounts the time he lined up alongside him in a centenary match in London. 'I played for a Rest of the World side at Wembley, when I was at Barcelona, all the great players like (Michel) Platini on the pitch were all totally in awe of him,' he told BT Sport. "The first thing he did in the dressing room was sit there in just a pair of shorts, juggling his socks on his left foot for about five minutes. Then he went out on the pitch and did something incredible, one of the most unbelievable things I have even seen on a football pitch. He juggled the ball all the way out to the centre circle, when he got there, still juggling, he went 'bang' and kicked the ball up as high as he could, then waited. It came down, he went 'bang' and did it again. He did it 13 times and the most he ever did was walk three paces to it. All of us were sitting there saying: 'that is impossible'. I remember going to training the next day at Barcelona. We all tried it and the best anyone did was three and they were running for the third one. I've never seen anyone have such a beautiful affection with a football."

Lineker recounted a hilarious story from the last time he met Maradona. "He had a lovely sense of humour. I did the World Cup draw, the last time I saw him, in Moscow. We went through the draw and I had a little joke at his expense about picking the balls out, saying he's quite good with his hands. He thought it was really funny. It was quite a complex presentation. At the end of it, he came up to me and he said, 'Gary, Gary, that was amazing, you did a fantastic job'. I said, 'thanks, Diego'. He said, 'you know Gary, as a footballer, you were okay, but as a presenter doing this… if you were as good at football as you are at presenting, you might have been nearly as good as me!'"

Lineker dubbed Maradona's second strike against England as the greatest goal he has ever seen on a football pitch. Lineker added that it was even more remarkable that Maradona created that second goal against England considering the quality of the pitch as he remarked: "On a playing surface that was so poor, to do what he did was truly extraordinary. It was the only time in my career where I genuinely felt that I ought to put my hands together and applaud that goal. A part of me was also gutted. It was definitely the best thing I've ever seen on a football pitch. It's the best goal that's ever been scored. You see great goals every now and again, I've seen [Lionel] Messi score very similar to that, but it was in a La Liga game, not in a quarter-final of a World Cup against England on a dodgy pitch. Some of the things he could do were truly breathtaking. It was almost like he'd been planted down from some other planet."

Paul Gascoigne once asked Maradona for a lighter at a Soccer Aid match in Manchester in 2006 when they faced each other in the annual charity match at Old Trafford. "At a charity game, I remember I wanted a lighter. I'd seen a little fella outside with a parka hat on, smoking a big long cigar," he told ITV's *Good Morning Britain*. "I just went up from behind him and I just said 'can I borrow you lighter please'. And he turned round and it was Diego, so I started laughing. So I shared a bit of his cigar with him. And we clicked then."

The pair had actually met 14 years earlier. Gazza's Lazio faced Maradona's Sevilla at the Ramon Sanchez Pizjuan Stadium in 1992. Gazza added, "My icon is Bryan Robson, but round the world Diego was just a phenomenal footballer, wasn't he."

Peter Beardsley, Peter Reid, Terry Fenwick and Terry Butcher were all beaten by that dazzling dribble from Maradona to score the greatest ever World Cup goals. Butcher, in fact, is beaten twice. "That's the closest I ever got to him on the pitch apart from the doping room after the game," Butcher has since said. Peter Reid admitted he still has nightmares. "In my dreams, I'm still running but there's a wind against me," he has recalled. "No matter how hard I try, I can't get there." Even Peter Shilton has to appreciate its majesty. "In scoring that solo goal, he proved to the watching world that he was one of the all-time great footballers." In fairness to Shilton, he has never denied that greatness, despite never forgiving the Hand of God goal against him.

Steve Hodge, whose sliced clearance sent the ball back towards

England's goal and into Maradona's path, at least walked away with his shirt, "Suffice to say, I wasn't too pleased with this," Reid recalled. "I gave Hodgey the biggest bollocking he's ever had in his life. I never knew a single football match could have such a lasting effect on my life. It still hurts that he finished us off with his feet after opening the scoring with his hand – and I have had to come to terms with the fact that I may never get over it."

Maradona got the better of Butcher on and off the pitch. Butcher was in an anteroom deep inside the Azteca Stadium, a disconsolate figure awaiting a drugs test, feeling a deep sense of injustice and a grievance over the Hand of God. Suddenly, Maradona burst into the room and, without any hint of remorse then, the Argentine captain claimed via sign language that he had beaten Peter Shilton with a header before conjuring up the greatest goal ever scored. One hour after full-time, with both goals still being replayed on TV screens around the world, Maradona declined an opportunity to confess. It only served to further enrage Butcher, Gary Stevens and Kenny Sansom. 'How would FIFA punish him now? I don't know but I would pay a few thousand pounds to be in that room after the match again,' Butcher once said. 'And with him there sat across from us. Let's just put it like that. The referee has to see it. He didn't. I think the official was from Tunisia. I don't think he would get away with it nowadays. It would be spotted in football today. He could get a retrospective ban but it wouldn't stop you being out the World Cup if they acted on the TV evidence. He'd done the deed.'

The intervening years failed to blunt Butcher's sense of injustice. 'I'm not so sad that I have thought about it every day,' he said. 'I haven't got a Maradona doll in the house to stick pins into. It's a good idea, right enough. I don't have a "Maradona room" in the house, let me put it that way. His attitude annoyed me. Long after the game, he didn't admit to what had happened. That day he came into the drugs-test room and celebrated. He was the last person we wanted to see. When I gestured to him - as I couldn't speak Spanish and he knew no English - to declare if he had used his head or his hand, he pointed to his head. I think he feared that because it was a small room and there were three Englishmen in there, he ought to take the safest option. That was the thing that irritated me. If he had come in and said that he used his hand, then I would have wanted to thump him only four or five times, rather than the usual 20. I didn't know at the time of the goal if he had handled the ball. Peter Shilton ran past me, as did Glenn Hoddle, and I followed them in the hope the referee would chalk it off for handball.'

Only a couple of weeks later, Butcher met Maradona again at a charity match in Pasadena when the big centre-half was called up to play for The Rest of the World side against the Americas - and scored from a Gordon Strachan cross in a 2-2 draw. 'Even then, Maradona haunted me because they won that one on penalties, although the alcohol was kicking in for us by then,' said Butcher. 'That was just before I signed for Rangers. I flew to Britain to meet Graeme Souness at an airport hotel in London. He signed me, even though I went to the wrong hotel. Then, when I came north, I discovered Scotland had more Argentina fans than there had been at the World Cup! I certainly saw more of their shirts here. Everywhere I went with Rangers, the opposition fans would chant "Argentina, Argentina". '

Butcher was asked whether Maradona's second goal could have been 'performance-enhanced' given Diego's later problems in life? 'If he was on drugs, then I should have been on them, too, to try to combat it. I wouldn't comment on that,' replied Butcher. 'He did score an exceptional goal. I don't like to concede goals but, grudgingly, I have to admit that was a great goal. He beat me twice in that run; once at the start and then at the end. I blame others, though. Peter Reid was running on fumes by that time and once Maradona went past him, Peter just kept going out the stadium - his race was run. I didn't get a touch. I'd love to sit here and say that I got a touch and that it wasn't his goal - just to deprive him. But I couldn't get at the ball. I wish I'd scored the greatest own goal ever but I didn't. I tried and scored a few at Rangers after that, though.

"I will never forgive him. That's because it is not nice to lose under those circumstances. It was a great chance for England to win the World Cup. John Barnes came on and we had them on the rack for the last 15 minutes at 2-1 down. We should have played like that throughout. I regret we didn't. But it is not nice to exit like that. We built up momentum and felt 1986 could be our year.'

Butcher also insisted that Pelé remained his greatest player of all time. 'Maradona is the best I've played against, but the best I've seen is Pelé,' he said. 'It's not to do with what Maradona did in later life. Pelé is a decent ambassador for football. The way Pelé played, the goals he scored in World Cups and everything else, stands out more for me than Maradona.'

Butcher was one of the most vociferous voices in the England dressing condemning Maradona for his Hand of God goal, but he was to suffer again at the hands of his old adversary. Maradona collected his first win of his reign as Argentina manager with a 1-0 win over Butcher's Scotland on a night when the ex-England skipper stuck to his promise not to shake his hand. Asked whether he would shake Maradona's hand before that game, Butcher replied: 'I don't know. I am not bothered about that. For me, shaking hands with Maradona is not a focal point.' When asked later if he and his old rival had buried the hatchet behind the scenes Maradona dismissed Butcher with a stinging put-down. Maradona met Butcher's boss, George Burley, ahead of the friendly and the pair embraced warmly on the final whistle as Maradona celebrated victory thanks to an early strike from Maxi Rodriguez. But when asked if he had bumped into Butcher, Maradona said: "Who is Butcher? I greeted the manager of Scotland tonight - who is this guy Butcher you talk about?" Maradona was shuttled from Hampden to a waiting jet at Glasgow Airport to fly to the bedside of his pregnant daughter in a Madrid hospital but he broke out in a huge grin and added: "Since all this news about my daughter, this is the first time I've managed to laugh."

Brazilian legend Ronaldo spoke emotionally about his relationship with Diego. Ronaldo, who is now president of Spanish club Real Valladolid, spoke about Maradona at a press conference about the two being extremely close. He said: "Diego left an incredible legacy in football. His loss is very hard to take. The news caught me by surprise and left me very sad. I want to send my love to his family. He changed the lives of many people and I will always be eternally grateful for the inspiration he provided me." Ronaldo told an anecdote about Maradona which explained why he took to wearing two watches, one on each wrist. "One of the first times he came to visit me in Madrid we had dinner, Diego brought two watches and the legend went that he did not go anywhere without them both. I asked him why he wore two, and he said that his daughter had given them to him as a present and since then he had never taken them off. At the end of the meal he took one off and gave it to me as a gift. I didn't want to accept it, but he got angry and I was left with no choice. I will look after it for the rest of my life as a reminder of his generosity and friendship."

Three-time Grand Slam tennis champion and football loving Andy Murray met Maradona in London. He wrote on Instagram: "I was lucky enough to meet Maradona once at the 02 Arena. He had come to watch the tennis there. He spoke to me for a couple of minutes in Spanish with unbelievable energy, passion and expression. Unfortunately I barely understood a word but that didn't seem to matter. He was diminutive in size but clearly a larger than life character/personality with a ton of charisma. The following day I was given a signed Argentina (shirt) which he left for me that you can see in the second picture which reads: "To my friend Andy with all my love and hope that you soon become #1". 'Numero uno were the only words I understood from our conversation.' Murray finally became world No 1 in 2016.

Maradona had visited Manchester United during Sir Alex Ferguson's reign in 2008, an occasion recalled by Dimitar Berbatov "In the world of football, Maradona was God. It's a tragic and terrible day for everyone connected with football. Everyone loved the way he used to play and the way he touched the ball, he was something else. I always remember the day he came to the training ground at Manchester United, we were doing some drills on the pitch and all of a sudden someone said, "Is that Maradona with the boss coming over?" Everybody stopped and froze, we were all watching God walk towards us. It was a great experience to meet him in person as well as watch him score the goals he did, he was out of this world. It's a sad day for everyone in football, I'm lost for words.'

Terry Fenwick, who had tried and failed to stop for the second goal, recalled "I belted him two or three times in that game and I thought "that's him done". He was off the pitch for four and a half minutes after I whacked him once,' Fenwick told TalkSport "And when I turned round he was warming up to come back on, I was thinking 'what the hell have I got to do to stop this man?' He was built like you wouldn't believe. He was a pit bull and he came back for more all the time. The ball was stuck to that left foot, you couldn't get it off him. I tried to intimidate him but he was always there, ready for more. I didn't say two words to him but he was chatting to me from start to finish. That was the confidence of the man. He knew he was better than the rest. What a player!" Fenwick went on: "We had a detail that whenever he was on the ball, the nearest man had to get at him quickly and liven him up."

Trevor Steven, who played the first 74 minutes of that last-eight clash in Mexico City, recalled, "The quarter-final of a World Cup played at 9,000 feet above sea level and in temperatures above 100 degrees Fahrenheit... playing in those conditions was a challenge in itself but when you look at the level he took the game to it was almost unbelievable. I certainly feel I admired him but I didn't know whether to like him or loathe him as an individual because of the effect his action had on England but also on that group of players and on myself personally. As time goes by, the feelings get diluted somewhat and the wounds heal. You could take Maradona for what he was - a genius footballer, a flawed genius with his lifestyle, but with his footballing ability he was out there on his own. Of all the great players around the world, no one could do what he could do. That (the Hand of God) was a split second thing but he had 15 years of professional football where he won the highest honours. So we need to remember him for those achievements rather than being very parochial or personal about that day way back in June 1986.'

114

THE SENSATION OF THE 1994 WORLD CUP

E ngland failed to qualify for the World Cup in the United States in 1994 after defeat in Rotterdam - the *Daily Mirror* headline the next day was 'The End of the World' and, while it felt like English football had hit rock bottom with Graham Taylor being forced to quit and the nation out of the tournament they had nearly won four years earlier, the reality was that the 1994 Finals in the States was a joy to cover as a chief football writer, without all the hassle involved of being an England camp follower, and the usual nightmare of the fans causing mayhem from time to time.

This was my first World Cup without the burden of the day to day intensity of an England camp and the freedom to pick and chose which matches to cover rather than concentrate totally on England and maybe fit in the opening game and the Final. For all the pre-World Cup hysteria about how sub-standard it would be in a country with little to no football heritage since the legacy of the New York Cosmos and the collapse of the NASL following the retirements of Pelé, Beckenbauer, Moore and Best, the tournament was a joy. By the end it seemed that perhaps the rest of the world had taught the Americans the joys of the greatest sport in the world!

World Cups were traditionally shared between the powerhouses of Europe and South America, but in opting for the USA, FIFA attempted to assuage some of the bad feeling left by the contempt with which they felt they had been treated by chairman Joao Havelange during their bid for the 1986 tournament. Havelange and the FIFA Committee had listened to an hour-long pitch by the Americans to take over that tournament from Columbia who had to withdraw for economic reasons but they had already decided it was going to be given to Mexico following the success of the 1970 tournament. Finally, in 1988, the Havelange accepted the US bid, acknowledging the huge potential for profits in the biggest economy in the world, albeit one with very little history of playing the world's favourite game.

Travelling with a few friends and colleagues proved to be a joy and it took us all over the States and to some wonderful locations. However, the fact that Diego Maradona was back leading the Argentina team ensured that this was never going to be a hassle-free journalistic assignment. Sure enough, following a spectacular performance in Argentina's opening group game against Greece and helping his country to another win against Nigeria, Diego tested positive for a banned substance causing the scandal of the tournament.

Maradona's decline had long been coming – following a positive test for cocaine after a Serie A fixture against Bari in March 1991, he had been was banned from all football for 15 months by FIFA. *El Diego* soon headed back to his homeland to see out his ban before signing for Sevilla in La Liga, where he was reunited with his World Cup-winning manager Carlos Bilardo. Maradona played 26 games for the Spanish side but his one-season spell there came to an abrupt end in a league game against Burgos when a chunky, unfit Maradona was substituted with half an hour to play. He ripped off his captain's armband, screamed at his manager and furiously headed straight for the tunnel. Maradona had been indulged far too much in Seville. One evening, he was stopped from entering a local nightclub because he wasn't wearing formal shoes. Maradona asked the bouncer, 'Who do you think you're talking to? People kill themselves to kiss these shoes'. After the Burgos game, Maradona told reporters that he was going to talk about his substitution with Bilardo 'man to man' if, he added, Bilardo was indeed a man. The pair clashed again shortly afterwards and Maradona punched Bilardo. "I'm going because they don't love me. But you know what I really love? To be with the gypsies."

It was a dark, extremely difficult period for Maradona. In Jimmy Burns' biography *Hand of God: The Life of Diego Maradona,* the plight of Maradona at this point reflects his reliance on substances. "As always when he's decided to snort cocaine at home, Maradona makes his way to the bathroom, in the dark so as not to disturb the children or Claudia. It is four o'clock in the morning. He is setting out the cocaine lines, one alongside the other, when he hears a gentle tap on the bathroom door. 'Dad, can I come in?' whispers a little girl's voice. It is his elder daughter Dalma. He is taken so much by surprise that he can hardly utter a word. He throws the cocaine into the toilet. 'What's wrong, Daddy, why are you like this and not asleep?' Dalma asks."

Trying to save his career, Maradona went home and tried to console himself in family and fishing. He found a new club, Newell's Old Boys, and when he was unveiled in typical chaos and hero worship, he strolled onto the pitch with Dalma and his other daughter Giannina, by his side. With Daniel Cerrini, hired to knock him into shape, now part of his team, he went on a binge of crash diets and vitamin supplements. Within weeks, he had lost 30lbs.

Argentina struggled to qualify for the USA. Losing 5-0 to Colombia in Buenos Aires was a particular low-point as Maradona watched with the rest of his country as a fan in the stands, just a week before Maradona arrived at Newell's. Argentina were humiliated by Colombia at Estadio Monumental – Freddy Rincon and Faustino Asprilla both scored twice with Adolfo Valencia adding another. In their own backyard, Argentina had been torn apart. *El Grafico*, the Argentinean magazine, appeared the following week with a black cover to mark the traumatic set back with the headline: 'Disgraceful'. During the game, the Argentine supporters began to chant Maradona's name.

Alfio 'Coco' Basile had taken over as manger and decided to stick with the squad that had won the previous two Copa Américas for their World Cup qualifying campaign, so their former captain found himself a continued frustrated spectator but Argentina en masse called for Maradona.

Basile had already called Diego up for a friendly against Brazil in February 1993 and a few days later he turned out again for a game against Denmark and was then ignored. Maradona was furious. "I wouldn't play for Basile again if he came begging on his knees," he said.

Now, following that disastrous 5-0 hammering by Columbia Basile was backed into a corner and forced into picking the talisman for the two-legged play-off against Australia. On 31 October 1993 Maradona played his first competitive game for his country in over three years in Sydney. On 37 minutes his marauding run down the right side was brought to an end but he won the ball back, turned onto his left foot and curled in a perfect cross for Abel Balbo to head home the opener. But Australia equalised just five minutes later and the game ended 1-1.

In the return, Gabriel Batistuta's cross was deflected, looping in at the far corner and somehow Argentina had squeezed through. Diego would lead his country in a fourth World Cup finals. Despite England not being at the finals, all the big hitters made it; Brazil, Germany, Italy, Holland, Spain and Argentina. At 33 and largely unimpressive in his brief appearances for Newell's, Maradona's revival was overstated. Yet, there was a renewed sense of optimism among Argentinians.

The build-up to the Finals was fraught - it wasn't a good sign when Maradona pulled out of the Argentine World Cup squad in February, citing too much pressure and he couldn't cope mentally with the expectation of the Argentine public. The press were camped outside his country house for two days, where Maradona had been trying to escape all the pressures that had been building up, demanding an explanation. He wanted to relax with friends. He asked the journalists to leave. They didn't. Maradona picked up an air rifle, aimed it at the front gates and shoot at the journalists. Four were injured and two sued him. The police were called and legal action was taken by the wounded.

As usual with Maradona, his actions divided opinion. Some questioned his sanity, some excused him anything. Yet again, he was a victim of circumstance, paying a high price for his celebrity, his genius, was the typical 'defence' from those who simply didn't want to believe his excesses.

The normal outcome for firing on members of the press would be a term in jail. Not, Diego. Not at this time. He escaped virtually Scot free. Certainly he was free to represent his country at the World Cup in America as the case didn't come to trial for nearly four years later. Maradona was eventually found guilty of assault with a weapon and was handed the 'soft' punishment of a suspended prison sentence of two years and 10 months. The ruling was specifically given to clear the way to travel to France in the World Cup where Maradona was lined up as a commentator for several television networks covering the competition. The journalists injured by Maradona said they would appeal because they considered the sentence too light. "But at least this exemplary case does show that there is justice for all," said reporter Daniel Talamoni, one of the four journalists who sued Maradona. "When the case began four years ago, everyone said it was impossible they would sentence a man idolised in Argentina and forgiven everything."

On the eve of the USA World Cup, Maradona was not burdened by a case that had been put on the back burner, and there were zero protests about that. Maradona was back at a World Cup, captaining his country. Shooting a journalist, a lack of fitness, in urgent need of weight-loss, his dependence on recreational drugs, all of his excesses were forgiven in the hope of one last act of glory and brilliance. After all Argentina were unbeaten since return.

Were FIFA aware of Maradona's drug taking prior to the tournament? Who knows? But all sorts of rumours were flying around, and back in those days FIFA were capable of almost anything. His age and a 15-month suspension for cocaine use in 1991-92 had led many to predict that he wouldn't make this tournament, but FIFA made an exception for him, and wheeled him out for his final goodbye and it looked as though he wasn't going to disappoint.

Despite only just managing to qualify Argentina were still among the favourites for the tournament - they often struggled

119

in qualification only to light up the actual tournament. Maradona scored a goal and an assist in the first-round victories over Greece and Nigeria, and showed some of his dazzling dribbling form of old.

Argentina's first group game was against Greece at the Foxboro stadium near Boston in front of 54,000 fans. Argentina had a useful squad and wouldn't be solely reliant on the ageing Maradona. They were outstanding against Greece and two-nil up at half-time thanks to the brilliance of Batistuta. Maradona was still capable of dictating the pace of the game, but he was noticeably a tad bigger around the midriff and a touch slower, so no longer had that burst of speed and incredible dribbles.

Then, around the hour mark, a succession of one-touch passes around the edge of Greece's penalty area saw the ball arrive at Maradona's left foot. He took one touch to kill the ball, one touch to get the ball out of his feet, and then the third saw the ball arrow into the top left corner, despite being surrounded by defenders.

But it was Diego's wild celebration that raised eyebrows - running to the sideline looking directly into the camera, his eyes bulging, and mouth wide he threw his head forward to the lens. He looked like a man possessed. The microphones pitch-side picked up his screams as his gold-chain bounced around his neck. The skin appeared tight around his face. It was a dark and menacing image shown around the world. FIFA must have been wondering, as we all were, whether that was because he was fuelled by drugs.

Maradona was substituted after 83 minutes, departing to a standing ovation. It was a glorious Argentina performance, albeit against a poor Greek team, which they had won 4-0 in convincing fashion with Batistuta completing his hat-trick, but for them, more importantly, Maradona had the look of a man possessed to win the World Cup rather than possessed with drugs. At least, one can imagine that is how they felt.

Next up were Nigeria who had quite a few players now plying their trade in the big European leagues, and unexpectedly went

1-0 up after only eight minutes. After 28 minutes the new golden boy of Argentine football, Claudio Caniggia had scored twice. The second one was set up by a quick free-kick from Maradona. Argentina won 2-1, virtually qualifying for the next round. Match commentator Clive Tyldesley commented: "Maradona again, oh they just can't get the ball off him. Can he get a goal? He deserves one. That should be a penalty, surely? Look at this. Nobody can say he is finished" but the drama all happened after the final whistle. Maradona left the field holding hands with a nurse who was responsible for taking the Argentine captain to the drug testing area. That was quite something unusual, in fact, I can't recall that ever happening before. The usual protocol was for the players to be selected at random and then led to a private room to be tested. Mardona hardly seemed fazed, as he smiled and waved to the crowd still clutching the medics left-hand.

Four days later, on 29 June, Sepp Blatter, announced: "Both analysis of the urine sample have proved positive. The player Diego Maradona of the Argentinian national team has therefore violated the conditions of the doping control regulations, in the match Argentina, Nigeria." He had tested positive for ephedrine and was given another 15 month ban from all football and excluded immediately from the World Cup squad.

The result of all this was a dash across the continent to attend that unscheduled press conference in Dallas. Such was the mad panic that while my travelling companions managed to retrieve their luggage when we landed in Dallas, mine didn't seem to want to appear at all. Not wishing to miss the big story I hot footed it to the media centre, with only clothes I stood up in. where the impromptu press conference with Maradona was taking place. His expulsion from the World Cup was global news and the world's media had descended on the Sheraton Park Plaza Hotel in Dallas and although we thought we had planned the journey to arrive in good time, by the time we got there, the place was packed and the best vantage point was an auxiliary room where the press conference was being piped through via a TV connection.

I'd seen some pretty high profile press conferences before; Ruud Gullit going home from the World Cup, Bobby Robson announcing he was signing for PSV Eindhoven before leaving for Italia '90 but all of them paled into insignificance by comparison to this. There was pandemonium with a mass of hands holding microphones and shouting questions at a volume which I had never heard before at a media event.

For his part, Maradona was full of denial and complaint as he tried to explain away the evidence that he had been using banned drugs to lose weight at an unnatural rate to get himself into shape for his World Cup swan song. Maradona's part in the 1994 World Cup was painful and controversially short. His playing time for the tournament restricted to two appearances, totalling 173 minutes.

Maradona was abruptly removed from the World Cup having tested positive for five variants of ephedrine, a stimulant banned by FIFA. The decision was announced at a news conference six hours before Argentina played Bulgaria at the Cotton Bowl, a game they lost 2-0. I was there to witness the Maradona-less defeat. It would have been a record 22nd World Cup appearance for the 33-year-old, his country's captain and talisman, and their only hope of winning the tournament. The decision to remove Maradona from the World Cup was technically made by the Argentine soccer federation, which spared itself any further sanctions with their pre-emptive decision. FIFA then said at the time it would reserve a judgement on any further punishment of Maradona until after the World Cup ended.

Surrounded by the world's media, Maradona cut a broken figure, he talked quietly, taking pauses between answers. His brow furrowed, head bowed, tired, defeated. He didn't raise his voice, he was calm, calculated, composed but he was desperate. "They've [FIFA] cut my legs off. This is a real dirty business. I'd like to believe in Havelange and Blatter but after this...well, I don't want to say anything." He hinted at wider conspiracy, darker forces had sabotaged his World Cup. That he had been duped, conned, stabbed in the back. He believed others had failed him.

122

In Argentina, Maradona still had the support of his people. "The jury is still out as to whether he was treated unfairly by FIFA and the USA organising committee, but I don't think Maradona failed to take responsibility for his actions at all," Mora y Araujo, South American football specialist, commented. "Many Argentines revere him, particularly his playing days, but as he has survived many stumbles and picked up and carried on he has become increasingly human. So people are able to both admire and idolise him as the greatest player there ever was and take him with a pinch of salt. And as for who is to blame for the ephedrine incident? Well, probably Maradona, his medics, and FIFA/US organising committee in equal measure. Probably. A thorough poll might indicate otherwise, but that's my guess."

Ephedrine is a performance-enhancer. Asthmatics take it to clear their respiratory system. It can aid weight-loss. In the days leading up to Argentina's second Group D World Cup game against Nigeria in Boston, Maradona had been struggling with a cold, bunged up with a blocked nose and sought the help of 'The Prof' to give him something for it. Here was Maradona's detailed explanation of why he didn't believe he was taking performance enhancing drugs on FIFA's banned list.

The 'Prof' was Fernando Signorini, his long-time trainer. Together with Daniel Cerrini, they supervised Maradona's personal fitness regime for twelve months prior to the World Cup as Maradona was in urgent need of getting back into shape after all of his excesses first in Naples, but mostly in Seville. He was overweight and clearly unhappy with his level of fitness going into a World Cup, knowing he wouldn't be capable of doing himself justice without a crash diet and fitness regime. He was introduced to Cerrini, a bodybuilder, and happily engaged in extreme diets, vitamin supplements and extra training. He began to get back into shape and to feel good again and Cerrini was now an integral part of Maradona's 'inner circle' but Cerrini had been involved in a doping scandal in 1989 and Signorini was suspicious of the potential influence on a vulnerable Maradona.

He worried about Cerrini's short-term approach to Maradona's weight-loss and feared Cerrini placed far too much emphasis on how well Maradona looked rather than how he'd play in the searing, energy-sapping American summer.

Before he left for the US, Maradona said: "I am tired of all those who said I was fat and no longer the great Maradona. They will see the real Diego at the World Cup."

When the FIFA World Cup Organising Committee met in Zurich to decide Maradona's fate, they concluded that he didn't consciously take the drug to enhance his performance. FIFA, inevitably, looked at Maradona's previous indiscretions and his on-going battle with drugs when making their decision. Cerrini was also held accountable and both received fifteen-month bans from football. However, before the Nigerian game, Maradona had taken an assortment of drugs to alleviate his sinus problem, his weight issues and his diet.

Basile's team, shorn of Maradona, and deflated by the consequences of what had happened, did not win another game at the tournament. They lost their remaining group game 2-0 to Bulgaria before going out in the next round after losing 3-2 to Romania.

Never has a player been so worshipped and vilified in equal measure. In 1995, Eric Cantona expressed his admiration for Maradona. "In the course of time, it will be said that Maradona was to football what Rimbaud was to poetry and Mozart to music". The genius of Maradona came to an astonishing end on that fateful day on June 30th 1994.

Later, Maradona would say that drugs were 'practically brought to me on a tray'. According to Marcela Mora y Araujo, when "A book about the entire ephedrine incident, *El Ultimo Maradona,* was launched, during the presentation, the event was described as "the saddest day in Argentina". The Argentine camp was aware of Maradona's delicate condition and his work with Cerrini – the diets, the vitamins. Maradona possessed far too much influence. Finally, he admitted it to himself, that really he was the only one to blame. After flying home with the team Maradona said: 'I'm the only one responsible'. Yet, deep down that sense of betrayal lingered, he continued to believe he had been double-crossed by those around him who had used his name and profile to further their own career.

"A nation cannot be defined by a single event, and certainly not by this one," Mora y Araujo reflects. "I think Argentina – a country with over 30 million people – exhibits much of the traits and conflicting views as most other groups of humans. Socially, economically, and politically it has known both turmoil and bonanzas, but in terms of football the overall outcome is mostly positive."

Maradona scored 34 goals in 91 games for his country, but that record could have been so much more impressive. Yet, he fulfilled his destiny in winning the World Cup in 1986 and his legacy remains one of demi-god like status in his homeland, and for much of southern Italy centred around Naples. Having single-handedly to that 1986 triumph and sparked the team four years later by reaching the final, the end in Dallas meant the end of his country as a force in international football – they haven't won a tournament since he retired.

As for my luggage... well, it took two days to retrieve from the airport! Nothing was easy when Diego Maradona was involved!

CAREER SUMMARY

	League		Cup		Continental		Other		Total	
	APPS	GLS	APPS	GLS	APPS	GLS	APPS	GLS	APPS	GLS
ARGENTINOS JUNIORS										
1976	11	2	–	–	–	-	-	-	11	2
1977	49	19	–	–	–	-	-	-	49	19
1978	35	26	–	–	–	-	-	-	35	26
1979	26	26	–	–	–	-	-	-	26	26
1980	45	43	–	–	–	-	-	-	45	43
Total	166	116	–	–	–	-	-	-	166	116
BOCA JUNIORS										
1981	40	28	–	–	–	-	-	-	40	28
BARCELONA										
1982–83	20	11	5	3	4	5	6	4	35	23
1983–84	16	11	4	1	3	3	–		23	15
Total	36	22	9	4	7	8	6	4	58	38
NAPOLI										
1984–85	30	14	6	3	–	–			36	17
1985–86	29	11	2	2	–	–			31	13
1986–87	29	10	10	7	2	0	–		41	17
1987–88	28	15	9	6	2	0	–		39	21
1988–89	26	9	12	7	12	3	–		50	19
1989–90	28	16	3	2	5	0	–		36	18
1990–91	18	6	3	2	4	2	1[r]	0	26	10
Total	188	81	45	29	25	5	1	0	259	115
SEVILLA										
1992–93	26	5	3	3	–		–		29	8
NEWELL'S OLD BOYS										
1993–94	5	0	–	–	–				5	0
BOCA JUNIORS										
1995–96	24	5	–	–	–				24	5
1996–97	1	0	–	–	1	0			2	0
1997–98	5	2	–	–	–				5	2
Total	70	35	–	–	1	0			71	35
	491	259	57	36	32	13	8	4	588	312

BARCELONA

1982-83

Sep 4, 1982	Valencia	FC Barcelona	2:1	1
Sep 11, 1982	FC Barcelona	Real Valladolid CF	3:0	1
Sep 19, 1982	Sevilla FC	FC Barcelona	0:0	
Sep 25, 1982	FC Barcelona	Real Zaragoza	1:1	
Oct 9, 1982	FC Barcelona	RCD Espanyol	1:0	
Oct 17, 1982	CD Málaga	FC Barcelona	1:4	1
Oct 24, 1982	FC Barcelona	Sporting Gijón	1:1	
Oct 30, 1982	Racing	FC Barcelona	0:4	1
Nov 6, 1982	FC Barcelona	UD Salamanca (liq.)	3:0	
Nov 10, 1982	Real Betis	FC Barcelona	1:1	
Nov 21, 1982	FC Barcelona	Celta de Vigo	2:2	1
Nov 27, 1982	Real Madrid	FC Barcelona	0:2	
Dec 5, 1982	FC Barcelona	Real Sociedad	1:0	1
Mar 12, 1983	FC Barcelona	Real Betis Balompié	1:1	
Mar 20, 1983	Celta de Vigo	FC Barcelona	0:4	
Mar 26, 1983	FC Barcelona	Real Madrid	2:1	1
Apr 2, 1983	Real Sociedad	FC Barcelona	1:0	
Apr 10, 1983	Athletic	FC Barcelona	3:2	1
Apr 17, 1983	FC Barcelona	UD Las Palmas	7:2	3
May 1, 1983	CA Osasuna	FC Barcelona	1:0	

EUROPEAN CUP WINNERS' CUP

Sep 15, 1982	R1 L1	FC Barcelona	Apollon Limassol	8:0	3
Oct 20, 1982	L16 L1	Red Star	FC Barcelona	2:4	2
Nov 3, 1982	L16 L2	FC Barcelona	Red Star Belgrade	2:1	
Mar 16, 1983	QF 2L	FC Barcelona	Austria Vienna	1:1	

1983/84

| Sep 4, 1983 | Sevilla FC | FC Barcelona | 3:1 | |
| Sep 10, 1983 | FC Barcelona | CA Osasuna | 1:0 | |

127

Sep 18, 1983		RCD Mallorca	FC Barcelona	1:4	1
Sep 24, 1983		FC Barcelona	Athletic Bilbao	4:0	
Jan 8, 1984		FC Barcelona	Sevilla FC	3:1	2
Jan 15, 1984		CA Osasuna	FC Barcelona	4:2	2
Jan 22, 1984		FC Barcelona	RCD Mallorca	1:1	
Jan 29, 1984		Athletic	FC Barcelona	1:2	2
Feb 5, 1984		FC Barcelona	Real Murcia CF	2:0	
Feb 12, 1984		Sporting Gijón	FC Barcelona	0:0	
Feb 18, 1984		FC Barcelona	Real Valladolid CF	5:0	2
Feb 25, 1984		Real Madrid	FC Barcelona	2:1	1
Mar 17, 1984		FC Barcelona	Valencia CF	0:0	
Apr 7, 1984		Real Zaragoza	FC Barcelona	0:1	
Apr 15, 1984		FC Barcelona	UD Salamanca (liq.)	2:0	1
Apr 22, 1984		FC Barcelona	RCD Espanyol	5:2	

EUROPEAN CUP WINNERS' CUP

Sep 14, 1983	1R 1L	1.FC Magdeburg	FC Barcelona	1:5	3
Mar 7, 1984	QF 1L	FC Barcelona	Manchester United	2:0	
Mar 21, 1984	QF 2L	Man Utd	FC Barcelona	3:0	

NAPOLI

1984/85

Sep 16, 1984	Hellas Verona	SSC Napoli	3:1	
Sep 23, 1984	Napoli	UC Sampdoria	1:1	1
Sep 30, 1984	Torino	SSC Napoli	3:0	
Oct 7, 1984	Napoli	Como Calcio	3:0	1
Oct 14, 1984	Lazio	SSC Napoli	1:1	1
Oct 21, 1984	Napoli	Milan AC	0:0	
Oct 28, 1984	Atalanta	SSC Napoli	1:0	
Nov 11, 1984	Napoli	US Avellino	0:0	
Nov 18, 1984	Ascoli	SSC Napoli	1:1	
Nov 25, 1984	Napoli	US Cremonese	1:0	

Dec 2, 1984	Inter	SSC Napoli	2:1	
Dec 16, 1984	Napoli	AS Roma	1:2	
Dec 23, 1984	Juventus	SSC Napoli	2:0	
Jan 6, 1985	Napoli	Udinese Calcio	4:3	2
Jan 13, 1985	Fiorentina	SSC Napoli	0:1	1
Jan 20, 1985	Napoli	AC Hellas Verona	0:0	
Jan 27, 1985	Sampdoria	SSC Napoli	0:0	
Feb 10, 1985	Napoli	Torino Calcio	2:1	1
Feb 17, 1985	Como	SSC Napoli	1:1	1
Feb 24, 1985	Napoli	SS Lazio	4:0	3
Mar 3, 1985	Milan	SSC Napoli	2:1	
Mar 17, 1985	Napoli	Atalanta BC	1:0	
Mar 24, 1985	Avellino	SSC Napoli	0:1	
Mar 31, 1985	Napoli	Ascoli Calcio 1898	1:1	1
Apr 14, 1985	Cremonese	SSC Napoli	1:1	
Apr 21, 1985	Napoli	FC Internazionale	3:1	
Apr 28, 1985	AS Roma	SSC Napoli	1:1	
May 5, 1985	Napoli	Juventus FC	0:0	
May 12, 1985	Udinese	SSC Napoli	2:2	2
May 19, 1985	Napoli	AC Fiorentina	1:0	
1985/86				
Sep 8, 1985	Napoli	Como Calcio	2:1	
Sep 15, 1985	AC Pisa	SSC Napoli	1:1	
Sep 22, 1985	Napoli	Atalanta BC	1:0	
Sep 29, 1985	Napoli	AS Roma	1:1	1
Oct 6, 1985	Lecce	SSC Napoli	0:0	
Oct 13, 1985	Fiorentina	SSC Napoli	0:0	
Oct 20, 1985	Napoli	AC Hellas Verona	5:0	1
Oct 27, 1985	Torino	SSC Napoli	2:1	1
Nov 3, 1985	Napoli	Juventus FC	1:0	1

Nov 10, 1985	Inter	SSC Napoli	1:1	1
Nov 24, 1985	Napoli	Udinese Calcio	1:1	1
Dec 8, 1985	Napoli	Milan AC	2:0	
Dec 15, 1985	Sampdoria	SSC Napoli	2:0	
Dec 22, 1985	Napoli	US Avellino	1:0	
Jan 5, 1986	Como	SSC Napoli	1:1	1
Jan 12, 1986	Napoli	AC Pisa 1909	0:1	
Jan 19, 1986	Atalanta	SSC Napoli	0:0	
Jan 26, 1986	AS Roma	SSC Napoli	2:0	
Feb 9, 1986	Napoli	US Lecce	1:0	
Feb 16, 1986	Napoli	AC Fiorentina	0:0	
Feb 23, 1986	Hellas Verona	SSC Napoli	2:2	2
Mar 2, 1986	Napoli	Torino Calcio	3:1	
Mar 9, 1986	Juventus	SSC Napoli	1:1	
Mar 16, 1986	Napoli	FC Internazionale	1:0	1
Mar 23, 1986	Udinese	SSC Napoli	2:0	
Apr 6, 1986	Napoli	AS Bari	1:0	
Apr 13, 1986	Milan	SSC Napoli	1:2	1
Apr 20, 1986	Napoli	UC Sampdoria	3:0	
Apr 27, 1986	Avellino	SSC Napoli	0:1	
1986/87				
Sep 14, 1986	Brescia	SSC Napoli	0:1	1
Sep 21, 1986	Napoli	Udinese Calcio	1:1	
Sep 28, 1986	Avellino	SSC Napoli	0:0	
Oct 5, 1986	Napoli	Torino Calcio	3:1	
Oct 12, 1986	Sampdoria	SSC Napoli	1:2	1
Oct 19, 1986	Napoli	Atalanta BC	2:2	1
Oct 26, 1986	AS Roma	SSC Napoli	0:1	1
Nov 2, 1986	Napoli	FC Internazionale	0:0	
Nov 9, 1986	Juventus	SSC Napoli	1:3	

Nov 23, 1986		Napoli	FC Empoli	4:0	1
Nov 30, 1986		Napoli	AC Hellas Verona	0:0	
Dec 14, 1986		Milan	SSC Napoli	0:0	
Dec 21, 1986		Napoli	Como Calcio	2:1	
Jan 4, 1987		Fiorentina	SSC Napoli	3:1	1
Jan 11, 1987		Napoli	Ascoli Calcio 1898	3:0	
Jan 18, 1987		Napoli	Brescia Calcio	2:1	
Feb 1, 1987		Udinese	SSC Napoli	0:3	2
Feb 22, 1987		Torino	SSC Napoli	0:1	
Mar 1, 1987		Napoli	UC Sampdoria	1:1	1
Mar 8, 1987		Atalanta	SSC Napoli	0:1	
Mar 15, 1987		Napoli	AS Roma	0:0	
Mar 22, 1987		Inter	SSC Napoli	1:0	
Mar 29, 1987		Napoli	Juventus FC	2:1	
Apr 5, 1987		FC Empoli	SSC Napoli	0:0	
Apr 12, 1987		Hellas Verona	SSC Napoli	3:0	
Apr 26, 1987		Napoli	Milan AC	2:1	1
May 3, 1987		Como	SSC Napoli	1:1	
May 10, 1987		Napoli	AC Fiorentina	1:1	
May 17, 1987		Ascoli	SSC Napoli	1:1	
UEFA CUP					
Sep 17, 1986	1R 1L	Napoli	FC Toulouse	1:0	
Oct 1, 1986	1R 2L	Toulouse	SSC Napoli	0:1*	
	* Toulouse win 5-3 on pens				
1987/88					
Sep 13, 1987		Cesena	SSC Napoli	0:1	
Sep 20, 1987		Napoli	Ascoli Calcio 1898	2:1	
Oct 4, 1987		Avellino	SSC Napoli	0:1	
Oct 11, 1987		Napoli	Delfino Pescara 1936	6:0	1
Oct 25, 1987		AS Roma	SSC Napoli	1:1	

Nov 1, 1987		Napoli	FC Empoli	2:1	2
Nov 8, 1987		Como	SSC Napoli	0:0	
Nov 22, 1987		Napoli	Torino Calcio	3:1	1
Nov 29, 1987		Inter	SSC Napoli	1:1	
Dec 13, 1987		Napoli	Juventus FC	2:1	1
Dec 20, 1987		Napoli	AC Hellas Verona	4:1	1
Jan 3, 1988		Milan	SSC Napoli	4:1	
Jan 10, 1988		Napoli	AC Fiorentina	4:0	1
Jan 17, 1988		Sampdoria	SSC Napoli	0:1	1
Jan 24, 1988		Napoli	AC Cesena	2:0	1
Jan 31, 1988		Ascoli	SSC Napoli	1:3	1
Feb 7, 1988		Napoli	AC Pisa 1909	2:1	1
Feb 14, 1988		Napoli	US Avellino	4:0	1
Feb 28, 1988		Pescara	SSC Napoli	0:1	
Mar 6, 1988		Napoli	AS Roma	1:2	
Mar 13, 1988		FC Empoli	SSC Napoli	0:0	
Mar 20, 1988		Napoli	Como Calcio	3:0	
Mar 27, 1988		Torino	SSC Napoli	0:0	
Apr 10, 1988		Napoli	FC Internazionale	1:0	1
Apr 17, 1988		Juventus	SSC Napoli	3:1	
Apr 24, 1988		Hellas Verona	SSC Napoli	1:1	1
May 1, 1988		Napoli	Milan AC	2:3	1
EUROPEAN CHAMPIONS CUP					
Sep 16, 1987	1R 1L	Real Madrid	SSC Napoli	2:0	
Sep 30, 1987	1R 2L	Napoli	Real Madrid	1:1	
1988/89					
Oct 9, 1988		Napoli	Atalanta BC	1:0	
Oct 23, 1988		Napoli	Pescara	8:2	2
Oct 30, 1988		Cesena	SSC Napoli	0:1	
Nov 6, 1988		Napoli	SS Lazio	1:1	

Nov 20, 1988		Juventus	SSC Napoli	3:5	
Nov 27, 1988		Napoli	Milan AC	4:1	1
Dec 4, 1988		Napoli	AC Fiorentina	2:0	1
Dec 11, 1988		Hellas Verona	SSC Napoli	0:1	
Dec 18, 1988		Napoli	Bologna FC 1909	3:1	2
Dec 31, 1988		AS Roma	SSC Napoli	1:0	
Jan 8, 1989		Torino	SSC Napoli	0:1	
Jan 15, 1989		Napoli	FC Internazionale	0:0	
Jan 29, 1989		Napoli	Ascoli Calcio 1898	4:1	2
Feb 5, 1989		AC Pisa	SSC Napoli	0:1	
Feb 12, 1989		Napoli	Como Calcio	3:2	
Feb 19, 1989		Atalanta	SSC Napoli	1:1	1
Feb 26, 1989		Napoli	US Lecce	4:0	
Mar 5, 1989		Pescara	SSC Napoli	0:0	
Mar 12, 1989		Napoli	AC Cesena	1:0	
Apr 16, 1989		Fiorentina	SSC Napoli	1:3	
Apr 30, 1989		Napoli	AC Hellas Verona	1:0	
May 14, 1989		Napoli	AS Roma	1:1	
May 21, 1989		Napoli	Torino Calcio	4:1	
May 28, 1989		Inter	SSC Napoli	2:1	
Jun 4, 1989		Napoli	UC Sampdoria	1:1	
Jun 18, 1989		Napoli	AC Pisa 1909	0:0	
UEFA CUP					
Sep 7, 1988	1R 1L	Napoli	PAOK Thessaloniki	1:0	1
Oct 5, 1988	1R 2L	PAOK Salonika	SSC Napoli	1:1	
Oct 26, 1988	2R 1L	Lok Leipzig	SSC Napoli	1:1	
Nov 9, 1988	2R 2L	Napoli	Lok Leipzig	2:0	
Nov 23, 1988	3R 1L	G. Bordeaux	SSC Napoli	0:1	
Dec 7, 1988	3R 2L	Napoli	Bordeaux	0:0	
Feb 28, 1989	4R 1L	Juventus	SSC Napoli	2:0	

Mar 15, 1989	4R 2L	Napoli	Juventus FC (aet)	3:0	1
Apr 5, 1989	SF 1L	Napoli	Bayern Munich	2:0	
Apr 19, 1989	SF 2L	Bayern Munich	SSC Napoli	2:2	
May 3, 1989	F 1L	Napoli	VfB Stuttgart	2:1	1
May 17, 1989	F 2L	VfB Stuttgart	SSC Napoli	3:3	

1989/90

Sep 17, 1989	Napoli	AC Fiorentina	3:2	
Sep 24, 1989	Cremonese	SSC Napoli	1:1	1
Oct 1, 1989	Napoli	Milan AC	3:0	1
Oct 8, 1989	AS Roma	SSC Napoli	1:1	1
Oct 22, 1989	Napoli	FC Internazionale	2:0	1
Oct 29, 1989	Genoa	SSC Napoli	1:1	1
Nov 5, 1989	Napoli	US Lecce	3:2	
Nov 19, 1989	Napoli	UC Sampdoria	1:1	1
Nov 26, 1989	Juventus	SSC Napoli	1:1	
Dec 3, 1989	Napoli	Atalanta BC	3:1	
Dec 10, 1989	Bari	SSC Napoli	1:1	
Dec 17, 1989	Napoli	Bologna FC 1909	2:0	
Dec 30, 1989	Lazio	SSC Napoli	3:0	
Jan 7, 1990	Napoli	Ascoli Calcio 1898	1:0	
Jan 14, 1990	Udinese	SSC Napoli	2:2	1
Jan 17, 1990	Napoli	AC Cesena	1:0	
Jan 21, 1990	Napoli	AC Hellas Verona	2:0	1
Jan 28, 1990	Fiorentina	SSC Napoli	0:1	
Feb 4, 1990	Napoli	US Cremonese	3:0	2
Feb 11, 1990	Milan	SSC Napoli	3:0	
Feb 18, 1990	Napoli	AS Roma	3:1	2
Mar 11, 1990	Lecce	SSC Napoli	1:1	
Mar 18, 1990	Sampdoria	SSC Napoli	2:1	
Mar 25, 1990	Napoli	Juventus FC	3:1	2

Apr 8, 1990		Atalanta	SSC Napoli	0:2	
Apr 14, 1990		Napoli	AS Bari	3:0	1
Apr 22, 1990		Bologna	SSC Napoli	2:4	1
Apr 29, 1990		Napoli	SS Lazio	1:0	

UEFA CUP

Sep 12, 1989	1R 1L	Sporting CP	SSC Napoli	0:0	
Sep 26, 1989	1R 2L	Napoli	Sporting CP	0:0	
		Napoli win 3:2 on pens			
Oct 17, 1989	2R 1L	FC Wettingen	SSC Napoli	0:0	
Nov 22, 1989	3R 1L	Napoli	SV Werder Bremen	2:3	
Dec 6, 1989	3R 2L	Werder Bremen	SSC Napoli	5:1	

1990/91

Sep 9, 1990	Lecce	SSC Napoli	0:0	
Sep 16, 1990	Napoli	Cagliari Calcio	1:2	
Sep 23, 1990	AC Parma	SSC Napoli	1:0	
Sep 30, 1990	Napoli	AC Pisa 1909	2:1	1
Oct 7, 1990	Genoa	SSC Napoli	1:1	
Oct 21, 1990	Napoli	Milan AC	1:1	1
Oct 28, 1990	Napoli	AC Fiorentina	1:0	
Nov 11, 1990	Bari	SSC Napoli	0:0	
Nov 18, 1990	Napoli	UC Sampdoria	1:4	
Nov 25, 1990	Inter	SSC Napoli	2:1	
Dec 2, 1990	Napoli	Torino Calcio	2:1	1
Dec 16, 1990	Napoli	SS Lazio	2:1	
Jan 6, 1991	Juventus	SSC Napoli	1:0	
Jan 20, 1991	Bologna	SSC Napoli	1:0	
Jan 27, 1991	Napoli	US Lecce	2:2	
Feb 10, 1991	Napoli	AC Parma	4:2	2
Feb 17, 1991	AC Pisa	SSC Napoli	1:1	
Feb 24, 1991	Napoli	Genoa 1893	1:0	

Mar 3, 1991		Milan	SSC Napoli	4:1	
Mar 17, 1991		Napoli	AS Bari	1:0	
Mar 24, 1991		Sampdoria	SSC Napoli	4:1	1

EUROPEAN CHAMPIONS CUP

Sep 19, 1990	1R 1L	Napoli	Újpesti TE	3:0	2
Oct 3, 1990	1R 2L	Újpest	SSC Napoli	0:2	
Oct 24, 1990	2R 1L	Napoli	S. Moscow	0:0	
Nov 7, 1990	2R 2L	S. Moscow	SSC Napoli	0:0*	

SPARTAK MOSCOW win 5-3 on pens

SEVILLA

1992/93

Oct 3, 1992	Athletic	Sevilla FC	2:1	
Oct 6, 1992	Sevilla FC	Real Zaragoza	1:0	1
Oct 17, 1992	Espanyol	Sevilla FC	1:1	
Oct 24, 1992	Sevilla FC	Cádiz CF	1:0	
Nov 1, 1992	Real Oviedo	Sevilla FC	1:1	
Nov 8, 1992	Sevilla FC	Rayo Vallecano	3:2	1
Nov 22, 1992	Celta de Vigo	Sevilla FC	1:2	1
Nov 28, 1992	Sevilla FC	Atlético Madrid	1:3	
Dec 6, 1992	Sevilla FC	CA Osasuna	0:0	
Dec 12, 1992	Real Sociedad	Sevilla FC	1:0	
Dec 19, 1992	Sevilla FC	Real Madrid	2:0	
Jan 3, 1993	CD Tenerife	Sevilla FC	3:0	
Jan 10, 1993	Sevilla FC	FC Barcelona	0:0	
Jan 17, 1993	Burgos CF	Sevilla FC	0:2	
Jan 24, 1993	Sevilla FC	Sporting Gijón	1:0	1
Jan 31, 1993	Sevilla FC	Albacete Balompié	2:1	1
Feb 6, 1993	Dep. La Coruña	Sevilla FC	2:0	
Feb 14, 1993	Sevilla FC	Valencia CF	2:2	
Feb 21, 1993	CD Logroñés	Sevilla FC	2:0	

Feb 28, 1993	Sevilla FC	Athletic Bilbao	3:1
Mar 14, 1993	Sevilla FC	RCD Espanyol	1:1
Mar 21, 1993	Cádiz CF	Sevilla FC	0:0
Apr 4, 1993	Sevilla FC	Real Oviedo	0:1
May 16, 1993	Sevilla FC	Real Sociedad	3:1
May 23, 1993	Real Madrid	Sevilla FC	5:0
Jun 13, 1993	Sevilla FC	Burgos CF	1:1

INTERNATIONAL CAREER

	Gls		Date	Venue	Opponent	Score	Competition
1	-		27-2-77	Buenos Aires	Hungary	5-1	
2	-		24-8-77	Buenos Aires	Paraguay	2-1	
3	-		31-8-77	Asunción	Paraguay	0-2	
4	-		19-4-78	Buenos Aires	Eire	3-1	
5	-		25-4-79	Buenos Aires	Bulgaria	2-1	
6	-		22-5-79	Bern	Netherlands	0-0	
7	-		26-5-79	Roma	Italy	2-2	
8	-		29-5-79	Dublin	Eire	0-0	
9	1	1	2-6-79	Glasgow	Scotland	3-1	
10	1	2	25-6-79	Buenos Aires	F.I.F.A.	1-2	
11	-	2	2-8-79	Rio de Janeiro	Brazil	1-2	CA
12	1	3	8-8-79	Buenos Aires	Bolivia	3-0	CA
13	1	4	30-4-80	Buenos Aires	Eire	1-0	
14	-	4	13-5-80	London	England	1-3	
15	-	4	16-5-80	Dublin	Eire	1-0	
16	3	7	21-5-80	Wien	Austria	5-1	
17	-	7	18-9-80	Mendoza	Chile	2-2	
18	-	7	9-10-80	Buenos Aires	Bulgaria	2-0	
19	1	8	12-10-80	Buenos Aires	Poland	2-1	
20	-	8	15-10-80	Buenos Aires	Czechoslovakia	1-0	
21	1	9	4-12-80	Mar del Plata	Soviet Union	1-1	
22	1	10	16-12-80	Córdoba	Switzerland	5-0	
23	-	10	1-1-81	Montevideo	West Germany	2-1	Gold Cup
24	1	11	4-1-81	Montevideo	Brazil	1-1	Gold Cup
25	-	11	9-3-82	Mar del Plata	Czechoslovakia	0-0	
26	-	11	24-3-82	Buenos Aires	West Germany	1-1	
27	-	11	14-4-82	Buenos Aires	Soviet Union	1-1	
28	-	11	5-5-82	Buenos Aires	Bulgaria	2-1	
29	-	11	12-5-82	Rosario	Romania	1-0	
30	-	11	13-6-82	Barcelona	Belgium	0-1	WC
31	2	13	18-6-82	Alicante	Hungary	4-1	WC

32	-	13	23-6-82	Alicante	El Salvador	2-0	WC
33	-	13	29-6-82	Barcelona	Italy	1-2	WC
34	-	13	2-7-82	Barcelona	Brazil	1-3	WC
35	1	14	9-5-85	Buenos Aires	Paraguay	1-1	
36	1	15	14-5-85	Buenos Aires	Chile	2-0	
37	2	17	26-5-85	San Cristóbal	Venezuela	3-2	WCQ
38	-	17	2-6-85	Bogotá	Colombia	3-1	WCQ
39	1	18	9-6-85	Buenos Aires	Venezuela	3-0	WCQ
40	-	18	16-6-85	Buenos Aires	Colombia	1-0	WCQ
41	-	18	23-6-85	Lima	Peru	0-1	WCQ
42	-	18	30-6-85	Buenos Aires	Peru	2-2	WCQ
43	1	19	14-11-85	Los Angeles	Mexico	1-1	
44	-	19	17-11-85	Puebla	Mexico	1-1	
45	-	19	26-3-86	Paris	France	0-2	
46	-	19	30-4-86	Oslo	Norway	0-1	
47	2	21	4-5-86	Tel-Aviv	Israel	7-2	
48	-	21	2-6-86	Cd.de México	South Korea	3-1	WC
49	1	22	5-6-86	Puebla	Italy	1-1	WC
50	-	22	10-6-86	Cd.de México	Bulgaria	2-0	WC
51	-	22	16-6-86	Puebla	Uruguay	1-0	WC
52	2	24	22-6-86	Cd.de México	England	2-1	WC
53	2	26	25-6-86	Cd.de México	Belgium	2-0	WC
54	-	26	29-6-86	Cd.de México	West Germany	3-2	WC
55	1	27	10-6-87	Zürich	Italy	1-3	
56	1	28	27-6-87	Buenos Aires	Peru	1-1	CA
57	2	30	2-7-87	Buenos Aires	Ecuador	3-0	CA
58	-	30	9-7-87	Buenos Aires	Uruguay	0-1	CA
59	-	30	11-7-87	Buenos Aires	Colombia	1-2	CA
60	-	30	16-12-87	Buenos Aires	West Germany	1-0	
61	1	31	31-3-88	Berlin	SovietUnion	2-4	
62	-	31	2-4-88	Berlin	West Germany	0-1	
63	-	31	12-10-88	Sevilla	Spain	1-1	
64	-	31	2-7-89	Goiânia	Chile	1-0	CA
65	-	31	4-7-89	Goiânia	Ecuador	0-0	CA
66	-	31	8-7-89	Goiânia	Uruguay	1-0	CA
67	-	31	10-7-89	Goiânia	Bolivia	0-0	CA
68	-	31	12-7-89	Rio de Janeiro	Brazil	0-2	CA

69	-	31	14-7-89	Rio de Janeiro	Uruguay	0-2	CA
70	-	31	21-12-89	Cagliari	Italy	0-0	
71	-	31	3-5-90	Wien	Austria	1-1	
72	-	31	8-5-90	Bern	Switzerland	1-1	
73	1	32	22-5-90	Tel-Aviv	Israel	2-1	
74	-	32	8-6-90	Milano	Cameroon	0-1	WC
75	-	32	13-6-90	Napoli	Soviet Union	2-0	WC
76	-	32	18-6-90	Napoli	Romania	1-1	WC
77	-	32	23-6-90	Torino	Brazil	1-0	WC
78	-	32	30-6-90	Firenze	Yugoslavia	0-0	WC
					Argentina win 3-2 on pens		
79	-	32	3-7-90	Napoli	Italy	1-1	WC
					Argentina win 4-3 on pens		
80	-	32	8-7-90	Roma	West Germany	0-1	WC
81	-	32	18-2-93	Buenos Aires	Brazil	1-1	
82	-	32	24-2-93	Mar del Plata	Denmark	1-1 (5)	
					Argentina win 5-4 on pens		
83	-	32	31-10-93	Sydney	Australia	1-1	WCQ
84	-	32	17-11-93	Buenos Aires	Australia	1-0	WCQ
85	1	33	20-4-94	Salta	Morocco	3-1	
86	-	33	18-5-94	Santiago	Chile	3-3	
87	-	33	25-5-94	Guayaquil	Ecuador	0-1	
88	-	33	31-5-94	Tel-Aviv	Israel	3-0	
89	-	33	4-6-94	Zagreb	Croatia	0-0	
90	1	34	21-6-94	Boston	Greece	4-0	WC
91	-	34	25-6-94	Boston	Nigeria	2-1	WC

	Gls	Date	Venue	Opponent	Score	Competition
1	-	27-2-77	Buenos Aires	Hungary	5-1	
2	-	24-8-77	Buenos Aires	Paraguay	2-1	
3	-	31-8-77	Asunción	Paraguay	0-2	
4	-	19-4-78	Buenos Aires	Eire	3-1	
5	-	25-4-79	Buenos Aires	Bulgaria	2-1	
6	-	22-5-79	Bern	Netherlands	0-0	
7	-	26-5-79	Roma	Italy	2-2	
8	-	29-5-79	Dublin	Eire	0-0	
9	1	1	2-6-79	Glasgow	Scotland	3-1
10	1	2	25-6-79	Buenos Aires	F.I.F.A.	1-2
11	-	2	2-8-79	Rio de Janeiro	Brazil	1-2	CA
12	1	3	8-8-79	Buenos Aires	Bolivia	3-0	CA
13	1	4	30-4-80	Buenos Aires	Eire	1-0
14	-	4	13-5-80	London	England	1-3
15	-	4	16-5-80	Dublin	Eire	1-0
16	3	7	21-5-80	Wien	Austria	5-1
17	-	7	18-9-80	Mendoza	Chile	2-2
18	-	7	9-10-80	Buenos Aires	Bulgaria	2-0
19	1	8	12-10-80	Buenos Aires	Poland	2-1
20	-	8	15-10-80	Buenos Aires	Czechoslovakia	1-0
21	1	9	4-12-80	Mar del Plata	Soviet Union	1-1
22	1	10	16-12-80	Córdoba	Switzerland	5-0
23	-	10	1-1-81	Montevideo	West Germany	2-1	Gold Cup
24	1	11	4-1-81	Montevideo	Brazil	1-1	Gold Cup
25	-	11	9-3-82	Mar del Plata	Czechoslovakia	0-0
26	-	11	24-3-82	Buenos Aires	West Germany	1-1
27	-	11	14-4-82	Buenos Aires	Soviet Union	1-1
28	-	11	5-5-82	Buenos Aires	Bulgaria	2-1
29	-	11	12-5-82	Rosario	Romania	1-0
30	-	11	13-6-82	Barcelona	Belgium	0-1	WC
31	2	13	18-6-82	Alicante	Hungary	4-1	WC
32	-	13	23-6-82	Alicante	El Salvador	2-0	WC
33	-	13	29-6-82	Barcelona	Italy	1-2	WC
34	-	13	2-7-82	Barcelona	Brazil	1-3	WC
35	1	14	9-5-85	Buenos Aires	Paraguay	1-1
36	1	15	14-5-85	Buenos Aires	Chile	2-0

37	2	17	26-5-85	San Cristóbal	Venezuela	3-2	WCQ
38	-	17	2-6-85	Bogotá	Colombia	3-1	WCQ
39	1	18	9-6-85	Buenos Aires	Venezuela	3-0	WCQ
40	-	18	16-6-85	Buenos Aires	Colombia	1-0	WCQ
41	-	18	23-6-85	Lima	Peru	0-1	WCQ
42	-	18	30-6-85	Buenos Aires	Peru	2-2	WCQ
43	1	19	14-11-85	Los Angeles	Mexico	1-1	
44	-	19	17-11-85	Puebla	Mexico	1-1	
45	-	19	26-3-86	Paris	France	0-2	
46	-	19	30-4-86	Oslo	Norway	0-1	
47	2	21	4-5-86	Tel-Aviv	Israel	7-2	
48	-	21	2-6-86	Cd.de México	South Korea	3-1	WC
49	1	22	5-6-86	Puebla	Italy	1-1	WC
50	-	22	10-6-86	Cd.de México	Bulgaria	2-0	WC
51	-	22	16-6-86	Puebla	Uruguay	1-0	WC
52	2	24	22-6-86	Cd.de México	England	2-1	WC
53	2	26	25-6-86	Cd.de México	Belgium	2-0	WC
54	-	26	29-6-86	Cd.de México	West Germany	3-2	WC
55	1	27	10-6-87	Zürich	Italy	1-3	
56	1	28	27-6-87	Buenos Aires	Peru	1-1	CA
57	2	30	2-7-87	Buenos Aires	Ecuador	3-0	CA
58	-	30	9-7-87	Buenos Aires	Uruguay	0-1	CA
59	-	30	11-7-87	Buenos Aires	Colombia	1-2	CA
60	-	30	16-12-87	Buenos Aires	West Germany	1-0	
61	1	31	31-3-88	Berlin	SovietUnion	2-4	
62	-	31	2-4-88	Berlin	West Germany	0-1	
63	-	31	12-10-88	Sevilla	Spain	1-1	
64	-	31	2-7-89	Goiânia	Chile	1-0	CA
65	-	31	4-7-89	Goiânia	Ecuador	0-0	CA
66	-	31	8-7-89	Goiânia	Uruguay	1-0	CA
67	-	31	10-7-89	Goiânia	Bolivia	0-0	CA
68	-	31	12-7-89	Rio de Janeiro	Brazil	0-2	CA
69	-	31	14-7-89	Rio de Janeiro	Uruguay	0-2	CA
70	-	31	21-12-89	Cagliari	Italy	0-0	
71	-	31	3-5-90	Wien	Austria	1-1	
72	-	31	8-5-90	Bern	Switzerland	1-1	
73	1	32	22-5-90	Tel-Aviv	Israel	2-1	

74	-	32	8-6-90	Milano	Cameroon	0-1	WC
75	-	32	13-6-90	Napoli	Soviet Union	2-0	WC
76	-	32	18-6-90	Napoli	Romania	1-1	WC
77	-	32	23-6-90	Torino	Brazil	1-0	WC
78	-	32	30-6-90	Firenze	Yugoslavia	0-0	WC
					Argentina win 3-2 on pens		
79	-	32	3-7-90	Napoli	Italy	1-1	WC
					Argentina win 4-3 on pens		
80	-	32	8-7-90	Roma	West Germany	0-1	WC
81	-	32	18-2-93	Buenos Aires	Brazil	1-1	
82	-	32	24-2-93	Mar del Plata	Denmark	1-1 (5)	
					Argentina win 5-4 on pens		
83	-	32	31-10-93	Sydney	Australia	1-1	WCQ
84	-	32	17-11-93	Buenos Aires	Australia	1-0	WCQ
85	1	33	20-4-94	Salta	Morocco	3-1	
86	-	33	18-5-94	Santiago	Chile	3-3	
87	-	33	25-5-94	Guayaquil	Ecuador	0-1	
88	-	33	31-5-94	Tel-Aviv	Israel	3-0	
89	-	33	4-6-94	Zagreb	Croatia	0-0	
90	1	34	21-6-94	Boston	Greece	4-0	WC
91	-	34	25-6-94	Boston	Nigeria	2-1	WC

Also available...